Lunkers, Keepers, and Ones that Got Away

Fish Tales, illustration by Sid Boyum. FRIENDS OF SID BOYUM, COURTESY OF THE WISCONSIN HISTORICAL SOCIETY. WHI IMAGE ID 121626

Lunkers, Keepers, and Ones that Got Away

Fish Tales from Four Generations of Anglers

Jerry Apps

WISCONSIN HISTORICAL SOCIETY PRESS

Published by the Wisconsin Historical Society Press
Publishers since 1855

The Wisconsin Historical Society helps people connect to the past by collecting, preserving, and sharing stories. Founded in 1846, the Society is one of the nation's finest historical institutions.
Join the Wisconsin Historical Society: wisconsinhistory.org/membership

© 2025 by Jerold W. Apps

For permission to reuse material from *Lunkers, Keepers, and Ones that Got Away* (ISBN 978-1-9766-0045-6; e-book ISBN 978-1-9766-0046-3), please access www.copyright.com or contact the Copyright Clearance Center, Inc. (CCC), 222 Rosewood Drive, Danvers, MA 01923, 978-750-8400. CCC is a not-for-profit organization that provides licenses and registration for a variety of users.

Photographs are from the author's collection unless otherwise credited. Photographs identified with WHi or WHS are from the Society's collections; address requests to reproduce these photos to the Visual Materials Archivist at the Wisconsin Historical Society, 816 State Street, Madison, WI 53706.

Front cover image adapted from a state of Wisconsin promotional poster titled "Wisconsin: Home of the Muskie" in the collections of the Wisconsin Historical Society, WHi image 79611; page v image: My father, Herman Apps, loved fishing.

Printed in Canada
Cover design by Ryan Scheife, Mayfly Design
Typesetting by Tom Heffron

29 28 27 26 25   1 2 3 4 5

Library of Congress Cataloging-in-Publication Data

Names: Apps, Jerry, 1934– author.
Title: Lunkers, keepers, and ones that got away : fish tales from four generations of anglers / Jerry Apps.
Other titles: Fish tales from four generations of anglers
Description: Madison, WI : Wisconsin Historical Society Press, [2025] | Includes bibliographical references and index.
Identifiers: LCCN 2024042376 (print) | LCCN 2024042377 (ebook) | ISBN 9781976600456 (paperback) | ISBN 9781976600463 (ebook)
Subjects: LCSH: Fishing—Wisconsin—Chain O' Lakes Region—Anecdotes. | Chain O' Lakes Region (Wis.)—Social life and customs. | Apps, Jerry, 1934– Family.
Classification: LCC SH563 .A67 2025 (print) | LCC SH563 (ebook) | DDC 799.109775—dc23/eng/20241002
LC record available at https://lccn.loc.gov/2024042376
LC ebook record available at https://lccn.loc.gov/2024042377

∞ The paper used in this publication meets the minimum requirements of the American National Standard for Information Sciences—Permanence of Paper for Printed Library Materials, ANSI Z39.48-1992.

*When my father, Herman, was ninety-three years old,
I asked him what he would have done differently in his long life.
He answered, "I would have spent more time fishing."*

Contents

Introduction	1
Commonly Caught Fish	4
1 You Wanna Go Fishing?	13
Fish Tale: Sue's Fishing Memories	
2 Of Poles, Rods, and Lures	17
Fish Tale: Winning Lure	
3 Ice Fishing in the Early Days	25
Fish Tale: Ice Fishing Memory	
4 Messing About in Boats (and Canoes)	30
Fishing Equipment Basics	36
5 Kids' First Fishing Adventures	39
Fish Tale: Not Only Fish Get Hooked	
6 Bullheads and Bluegills	46
Wisconsin's Oldest Fish	50
7 Opening Day	52
Fish Tale: Opening Day with Pa	
8 Fishing with Grandpa Apps	59
Fish Tale: "It's a Pole Bender!"	
The Language of Fishing	63
9 Fishing Weather	67
Fish Tale: Windy Day on the Bay	
10 All About Bait	72
Fish Tale: A Bait Idea	

11 Favorite Fishing Places   80
     Fish Tale: Surprise Catch

Fish on Our Plates   88

12 Boundary Waters Time   94

13 More Adventures on Ice   105
     Fish Tale: First Time Ice Fishing

14 Fishing with Friends   112
     Fish Tale: Fishing with Uncle Jim

Learning to Fly (Fish)   121

15 Misadventures and Near Disasters   124
     Fish Tale: Unexpected Fishing Hazard

16 Piscatorial Retreat   132

Lake Michigan Fish Tales   136

17 Grandkid Stories   142
     Fish Tale: Never Too Young

Wisconsin Fish Festivals   153

Epilogue   156
Acknowledgments   159
Source Notes   161
Index   163

Introduction

Growing up on a farm, we had little time for fishing during the warmer months. Our father always had something for my twin brothers and me to do, and the work grew as we got bigger. In spring we planted potatoes, oats, and corn. In summer there was hay to be cut, raked, piled into bunches, hauled to the barn with our trusty team of horses, and piled into the searing-hot haymow. When we weren't busy with those tasks, there were always potatoes to hoe—hour after hour of hoeing—and fences to repair.

But every so often, on a warm summer evening when the milking was done and the cows were turned out to pasture, Pa suggested we go fishing. Donald or Darrel would run to grab our cane poles from where they were tucked up under the corncrib eaves, with fishlines and bobbers already in place, and I would head to where the earthworms were waiting in the loose, rich soil behind the chicken house. Using a six-tine barn fork, I would dig

My brothers and I never turned down an opportunity to go fishing.

1

up a couple dozen fat, wiggly worms and drop them in an empty pork-and-beans can that Ma had saved for us.

With only a couple of daylight hours remaining for fishing, we hurried to tie the poles to the top of our 1936 Plymouth, wrapping binding twine around the front and rear bumpers to hold the poles in place. Then we were on our way down the dusty country road to Chain O' Lake, about a mile and a half from our farm. (Chain O' Lake is connected under the surface, like a chain, to several other spring-fed lakes, but locals know this particular lake is always called Chain O' Lake, singular.)

Pa turned onto a twisty road that snaked through the woods, and then we arrived at the lake. We were alone.

We untied the poles, and I grabbed the can of worms. There was an old wooden boat pulled up on shore that nobody ever seemed to claim. We clambered in with our gear and used the oars to push off. Pa rowed us out to the deepest spot in the lake, maybe twelve feet deep, where the water was cool and the perch and bluegills liked to hang out on warm summer days.

We baited our hooks and tossed our heavy green fishlines into that deep spot. Our red-and-white bobbers bobbed. The sun sank below the trees that lined the lake to the south and west. The occasional bullfrog let out a loud *har-umph*, and a whippoorwill called its name, again and again, from the south. I counted ten *whip-poor-wills*. Pa had always said we should be quiet when fishing—he believed the fish could hear us talking. I wasn't sure if that was true, but even so, my brothers and I ceased talking and listened to the sounds of an early summer evening.

On those trips to Chain O' Lake with Pa, my brothers and I learned how to fish, but we learned so much more. As we watched our bobbers on the smooth lake surface, waiting for the telltale tug on our line, we were immersed in the sights and sounds of nature. We learned lessons without realizing we were learning

Introduction

them, lessons like patience and persistence, problem-solving and resourcefulness. Lessons that have lasted a lifetime.

In this book I share fishing stories of four generations of my family, including stories told by my dad and brothers, my kids, and my grandkids. It's a long tradition among fishing folks to pass along tales told by others, so I also share stories that have come my way from extended family and friends.

In preparing to write this book, I drew on interviews with my brothers, Donald and Darrel; my children, Sue, Steve, and Jeff; and my grandchildren. I went back to my journals, which I have kept for many years and where I included fishing stories along with the other adventures in my life. I also relied on Outdoor Notebook, the weekly column I wrote for four central Wisconsin newspapers from 1967 to 1977.

Some of the stories are humorous, and some are serious (and some are a bit of both, like the time I fell out of the boat on opening day of fishing season). Along with stories, I share tips I have picked up over the years, including the equipment and bait I prefer, favorite fishing locations, fishing lingo, our family's most-often-eaten fish recipes, and more. And I discuss how fishing has influenced four generations of my family, instilling in each of us a love of the outdoors and appreciation of the wonders of nature.

Commonly Caught Fish

With more than fifteen thousand lakes and eighty-four thousand miles of rivers and streams, Wisconsin is home to an abundance of fish—more than 160 species, according to the Wisconsin Department of Natural Resources. Here are brief descriptions of the fish most commonly caught in Wisconsin, including each fish's habits and tips for anglers hoping to catch one.[1] The sturgeon, Wisconsin's oldest fish, is discussed on page 50.

LARGEMOUTH BASS

This scrappy fish is found throughout Wisconsin (though less frequently in the southwestern counties). It spawns from late April to early July, in a nest the male largemouth builds on the lake bottom. The largemouth bass will bite on nearly any bait anglers offer, whether artificial or natural. These fish are usually found in weedy areas. Best largemouth fishing times are in the early morning or the evening during the warm months of the year. They seldom bite in the winter. Wisconsin's record largemouth bass was 11 pounds, 3 ounces, caught in Lake Ripley in 1940.

SMALLMOUTH BASS

Smallmouth bass are found throughout Wisconsin, most often in medium to large streams and in large lakes. They spawn in a perfectly round nest on the bottom of a body of water. The male protects the nest from all intruders. Spawning takes place when the water temperature reaches sixty degrees or higher.

Commonly Caught Fish 5

For the angler, the smallmouth bass is one of the feistiest of all game fish, putting up a spectacular fight when it is hooked, diving and leaping into the air. Good times for fishing smallmouth are just after the spawning season in June or in early fall. Light tackle is an effective choice when fishing for this fighter; small spoons and spinners work well. Wisconsin's record smallmouth bass weighed in at 9 pounds, 1 ounce, and was caught at Indian Lake in 1950.

CATFISH

Catfish get their name from the whiskers on either side of their snouts. They prowl the bottoms of lakes and rivers, generally resting during the day and feeding at night. Catfish are not fussy eaters and

Wisconsin artist Sid Boyum (1913–1991) worked in many artistic forms, but he might be most remembered for the pen-and-ink illustrations he created to honor the annual opening day of fishing season. These humorous sketches ran from 1963 to 1989 in the *Capital Times* of Madison and the *Wisconsin State Journal* and reflected his love of fishing. Many of his opening day drawings and other illustrations, including this one, are part of the Sid Boyum Collection held by the Wisconsin Historical Society. FRIENDS OF SID BOYUM, COURTESY OF THE WISCONSIN HISTORICAL SOCIETY. WHI IMAGE ID 123643 will bite on most anything. They have a well-developed sense of smell, which helps them find their food. They are commonly found in the lower Mississippi and lower Wisconsin Rivers. The record catfish caught in Wisconsin weighed in at 44 pounds, caught on the Wisconsin River in 1962.

BULLHEAD

Bullheads are members of the catfish family and resemble miniature catfish. There are three subspecies: black, brown, and yellow bullheads. Like catfish, they have whiskers on each side of their snouts. They are found in warm water lakes throughout much of Wisconsin, except for the southwestern counties. Bullheads will bite on almost any bait, at most any time of day. They're such a common fish that many anglers grew up catching bullheads, experiencing the fun of having a fighting fish on the end of their line. Bullheads are tough and will live in waters where other fish species would perish. Fishery managers have little love for bullheads, which are known for stirring up the bottoms of lakes and spoiling the habitat for other fish species. They are also known for feeding on the spawn of other fish. They repopulate rapidly in small ponds and lakes, crowding out other fish species.

Records of the largest bullheads caught in the state include: black bullhead, 5 pounds, 8 ounces, 21.5 inches, Big Falls Flowage, 1989; brown bullhead, 4 pounds, 2 ounces, 17.5 inches, Little Green Lake, 2006; and yellow bullhead, 4 pounds, 2.3 ounces, 19.5 inches, White Mound Park Lake, 2020.

BLUEGILL

Bluegills are one of the most popular fish caught in Wisconsin. They are widely distributed in lakes throughout the state. They spawn from late May to early August; peak spawning occurs in June when water temperatures reach about seventy degrees. The male bluegill builds a nest on the lake's bottom, usually selecting a sand or gravel bar. Before and after spawning, the male bluegill can be found defending the nest. The best bait for bluegills is a wiggly earthworm, but they will bite on a variety of other baits and lures as well. In the spring, bluegills are most readily caught when they are over the nests. As summer warms the lake, they retreat to deeper water. The bluegill is also a prime panfish for ice fishers. Winter bait usually includes small wire worms and grubs. Pan-fried bluegills are a real treat.

Wisconsin's record bluegill weighed 2 pounds, 9.8 ounces, and was caught in Green Bay in 1995.

PUMPKINSEED

Fishing for these little fish is one good way to introduce children to fishing; pumpkinseeds frequent shallow water and thus are easily caught from shore with a cane pole and an earthworm for bait. A close relative of the bluegill, pumpkinseeds rarely are longer than eight inches, but they put up a good fight when hooked.

Pumpkinseeds are found throughout Wisconsin. They remain active throughout the day, especially in spring and summer, when they are defending their nests. The record pumpkinseed caught in Wisconsin weighed 1 pound, 3.5 ounces. It was caught in 2020 in Silver Lake.

BLACK CRAPPIE

The black crappie is found throughout Wisconsin, with the exception of the southwestern part of the state. Crappies spawn in May and June, sometimes in July if it has been a cold spring. The male crappie builds the spawning nest and defends it until the spawned little crappies are able to begin feeding.

The best baits for catching crappies are small minnows or lures. The bait must be kept moving. Crappies are usually found in deeper water. They tend to bite best in the early morning or early evening. Crappies are a popular fish for ice fishers; small minnows work best in winter. The record black crappie caught in Wisconsin weighed 4 pounds, 8 ounces, and was caught in Gile Flowage in 1967.

YELLOW PERCH

Yellow perch are known widely in Wisconsin not just as a popular fish for catching but as a tasty treat for eating. They are found throughout Wisconsin's waters, including Lake Michigan, Lake Superior, and the Mississippi River, but are typically not found in the unglaciated southwestern part of the state.

Perch usually spawn shortly after the ice is out in April or early May. They are random spawners and do not build nests or guard their eggs and young like some fish species do. Perch are bottom feeders and will bite on a variety of baits, including minnows and worms. Perch prefer cool water, so in summer, perch anglers head to deeper water. These small fish move in schools, so if you catch one, you are likely to catch another in the same place.

The record yellow perch caught in Wisconsin weighed in at 3 pounds, 4 ounces (length not recorded). It was caught on Lake Winnebago in 1954.

SMELT

Smelt are a silvery little fish, 4 to 7 inches long. They are nonnative, having arrived in the Great Lakes from the Atlantic Ocean; some stories claim they were planted in a Michigan lake in 1912 and from there made their way into Lake Michigan and the rest of the Great Lakes. Smelt are caught during the spring spawning, usually between late March and the end of April for Great Lakes smelt and the last two weeks of April for Lake Superior smelt. Anglers fish for smelt at night, dipping long-handled nets into brooks and streams. Smelt numbers peaked in the 1980s; in recent years the number of smelt have declined dramatically.[2]

Considered a delicacy, smelt have delicate skin and soft bones, so they can be eaten whole. Once the entrails are removed, the little fish can be broiled or baked. A common and delicious way of preparing them for the table is to dust them with flour and fry them.

NORTHERN PIKE

Northern pike are found throughout most of Wisconsin, except in the southwestern unglaciated area. They spawn as soon as the ice is out on the state's rivers and lakes, usually from late March to early May. Northern pike spawn in flooded areas; spawning usually

Commonly Caught Fish

My grandson Josh Horman caught this northern pike in Madison's Mud Lake in 2017.

involves one female and up to three males. The eggs are deposited on vegetation. Northern pike are most active when the water is cool. They are a predator fish and prefer live baits such as minnows and moving spoons. They are a common quarry for ice fishers, who use tip-ups to catch them.

Wisconsin's record northern pike weighed 38 pounds and was caught on Lake Puckaway in 1952.

MUSKELLUNGE (MUSKIE)

The legendary muskie is found throughout Wisconsin, most frequently in northern lakes and rivers. As a result of widespread stocking of fry and fingerlings, muskies can be found in many central and southern Wisconsin lakes as well. They grow to be huge and are great battlers when hooked, making them the prize fish for many anglers.

Muskies spawn from mid-April to mid-May when water temperatures reach fifty-five degrees. Unlike fish that spawn in beds on the bottoms of water bodies, muskies deposit their spawn for several hundreds of yards along a shoreline. Interestingly, adult muskie spawners return to the same spawning area in successive years.

Muskies are loners and sometimes hide in weed beds for protective cover. Muskie anglers do well when they fish during the daytime with large plugs, spoons, and bucktail artificial bait. Muskie will also go for large minnows, 10 to 12 inches long. The record muskie caught in Wisconsin was 69 pounds, 11 ounces, and 63.5 inches long. It was caught in the Chippewa Flowage in 1949.

WALLEYE

At one time, walleyes were found mainly in Wisconsin's larger lakes and waterways. They have been stocked extensively in many Wisconsin lakes, and today the fish is found throughout the state. Walleyes begin spawning shortly after the ice goes out in the spring, between mid-April and mid-May in waters with temperatures from thirty-eight to forty-four degrees. Spawning walleyes do not spawn in nests but usually merely scatter their eggs.

For many anglers, walleyes are the Cadillac of game fish. Successful walleye anglers use small artificial plugs as well as minnows, leaches, and nightcrawlers for bait. These fish are generally found in deeper water during the day. In the evening they move into shallower water. Walleyes have unusual, light-sensitive eyes that help them find their prey.

The record Wisconsin walleye weighed 18 pounds and was caught in High Lake in 1933.

BROWN TROUT

Brown trout, native to Europe, were brought to North America in the 1880s and over time were introduced to nearly all the lakes and streams in the United States. Brown trout will live in warmer and shallower water than their trout relatives. They have become a popular fish for anglers, but they can be a challenge, as they are wary and can be easily spooked.

Anglers can catch brown trout almost any time of year, including through the ice in winter. They are a fun fish to catch, no matter what type of fishing equipment is used. Many anglers catch them in early spring with light tackle, such as fly rods and flies. Browns will also go for small spoons and earthworms. The state record brown trout was 32 pounds, 8 ounces, caught in Lake Michigan in 1978.

RAINBOW TROUT

Rainbow trout are native to the Pacific Coast of North America. Today they are common in many Wisconsin waters, including Lake Michigan. When caught from Lake Michigan, rainbow trout are called steelheads. Rainbow trout are stocked in several states, a program supported by money collected from the sale of fishing licenses and Great Lakes Salmon and Trout Stamps.

Baits that attract rainbow trout include nightcrawlers and spoons of various types, as well as flies, plugs, and small minnows. In midsummer, steelheads are caught by anglers trolling far from shore using spoons or plugs.

Wisconsin's record inland rainbow trout weighed 12 pounds, 3 ounces, and was 29.5 inches long. It was caught in Elbow Lake in 2006.

BROOK TROUT

Brook trout are native to Wisconsin. This scrappy little trout can be found in the smallest of trout streams as well as in larger rivers and lakes. They spawn along shorelines and may repeat spawning each year for the five to six years of their lifespan. The eggs begin hatching when the water reaches forty-five degrees.

Anglers catch brook trout in streams and lakes during all seasons of the year. Ice fishers catch them in some of Lake Michigan's harbor areas. The best baits for brook trout include artificial flies, small spoons, spinners, and nightcrawlers. The record brook trout caught in Wisconsin weighed in at 9 pounds, 15 ounces, caught in the Prairie River in 1944.

LAKE TROUT

For thousands of years, lake trout lived in the Great Lakes with little or no change. By the 1880s, due to overfishing and pollution of spawning grounds, the seemingly endless supply of lake trout began declining. Fishing pressure increased, and the great stock of lake trout dwindled even further. Then, in the 1930s, the parasitic sea lamprey invaded the upper Great Lakes from the Atlantic Ocean to prey upon the remaining large fish. Lake trout nearly disappeared from Lake Michigan. Several state DNRs began restocking lake trout in Lake Michigan in the mid-1960s, a practice that continues today.

Lake trout mature at age six or seven when they are 24 to 28 inches long. They may live past twenty years. Anglers are most successful when they troll for lake trout with a plug or spoon at about eighty feet, as lake trout are usually found in deeper water. May to October are prime times for trolling for lake trout. Anglers fishing through the ice on inland lakes can also catch one of these prize fish.

Wisconsin's record lake trout caught on an inland lake was 35 pounds, 4 ounces, caught on Big Green Lake in 1957. The record lake trout caught in the Great Lakes weighed 47 pounds and was 42.5 inches long. It was caught in Lake Michigan in 1997.

CHINOOK SALMON

The chinook salmon is native to the Pacific Coast. It was introduced into the Great Lakes as early as 1867, but major stocking didn't occur until a hundred years later. The chinook has become one of the most popular fish for anglers on the Great Lakes. It is a big fish and a tremendous fighter. It is also very tasty. Today, most chinook salmon in the state begin their life in one of Wisconsin's fish hatcheries. Once in the lake, the fingerlings grow rapidly, reaching 18 inches within a year. For three to five years, the fish remain in the lake before returning to the stream where they were planted.

The chinook spends most of its life in the open lake, usually in water less than one hundred feet deep. For the angler, the best way to catch a chinook is by trolling with a plug or spoon, using a down-rigger to reach the fish. The best time to catch chinook is early June through October. Fishing is best in the early morning. The Wisconsin record for a chinook is 44 pounds, 15 ounces, and 47.6 inches long, caught in 1994 in Lake Michigan.

1

You Wanna Go Fishing?

When my brothers and I were too little to help with the heavy work on the farm, Pa employed a hired man, usually a young man in his late teens or early twenties, who lived with us for the summer and helped with whatever needed doing. It must have been about 1945, when I was eleven years old and Don and Darrel were seven, that Pa hired Henry Lackelt.

Henry drove a Model T Ford touring car. Today it would be called a convertible, as the top could be let down. On hot summer evenings, when the milking was done, Henry would ask, "You boys wanna go fishing?"

Of course we wanted to go fishing, every chance we got.

On those nights, we would gather up our fish poles, dig a few worms, and pile into that open-air Model T. What fun it was to go chugging down our dirt road, past the Millers' place, past the one-room school, to Chain O' Lake. It was most pleasant riding in the back of the old car, which could crank up to twenty or twenty-five miles an hour, creating a cooling breeze.

At the lake, Henry would back his Model T a couple yards into the lake. We all climbed up and sat on the back of the car, tossing our bobbers into deeper water. We fished until dark and then chugged our way back home. I don't remember if we caught many fish—perhaps a perch or two—but the experience was one I never forgot.

My brothers remember our boyhood fishing expeditions, too. Something about those experiences created lasting memories for all three of us. Like any memories, they have softened a bit with time, but they're still easy to call up and revisit, like turning the pages in the family scrapbook. What makes these memories of fishing so unforgettable? I suspect it's the combination of the physical and the emotional. When fishing, we were actively engaging with the natural world, using every part of our bodies and all our senses. At the same time, we were feeling the range of emotions that come with fishing, from excitement and wonder to occasional boredom, frustration, or disappointment. Sharing these experiences with family and close friends went even further to cement the moments in our memories.

Donald recalls, "One of my earliest memories of fishing was going to Bean's Lake with a cane pole on Memorial Day. The folks tended to the graves of our grandparents, the Witts, buried in the West Holden Church Cemetery. We caught bullheads and sunfish."

Darrel also remembers fishing at our nearby regular fishing spots, Chain O' Lake and Bean's Lake. He notes, "As a little kid, taking a hook out of a bullhead was a scary, unpleasant experience." And both brothers remember fishing trips to Norwegian Lake, where there were larger fish, such as black bass and northern pike. "Hooking a large fighting fish on a cane pole is not a comparable experience to using today's fancy flyrods," Darrel says.

Don can't forget the time we were ice fishing on Norwegian Lake and, as he tells it, "Darrel was swinging a tip-up around with a length of line with a hook attached. He caught the hook in my ear. We pulled the hook out of my ear and it bled like everything. Just then I had a bite on my tip-up. I bent over to attend to my tip-up while blood was dripping from my ear on the snow."

Fishing is a learn-by-doing activity. Fishing companions share their know-how, favorite gear, secret fishing spots, tried-and-true tips, and hard-earned lessons. Donald remembers one such lesson passed on by our cousin Harold Apps, who often went fishing with us on Norwegian Lake: "Harold said to catch bluegills, we should be using catgut, made from sheep intestines, not the heavy green braided line that we were using on our long cane poles. We tied some catgut on our lines, and we began catching bluegills, too."

Of course, along with the how-to lessons come plenty of what-not-to-do lessons. Donald tells this story of a lesson he learned one day while fishing with our dad—while also creating a memory he would never forget. "One time, when I was fishing with Pa on the Millpond," he explains, "we pulled our boat up on shore, and there stood a young assistant game warden. He said to me, 'You have more than your limit of fish. I've been watching you fish.'

"I said, 'If you can't tell a trout from a sucker, I've got too many fish.' That really ticked him off. He even looked in Pa's thermos bottle to see if he might have a fish stuck in there. We laid out all the fish for him to count. He finally walked away. I learned an important lesson while fishing with Pa. Don't catch more fish than the limit. You don't want to get pinched by a warden."

~ FISH TALE ~

Sue's Fishing Memories

My daughter, Sue, shares some of her fond memories of fishing and enjoying time in nature.

I remember sitting on the shore of our pond with my little fishing pole. I had trouble putting a worm on the hook. My dad taught me to thread the hook through the worm in several places. I felt so accomplished when I was able to do it! I learned how to cast the line out onto the pond, and I liked watching the little red-and-white bobber floating around. I also remember catching bullheads—one of them hit my leg, and its barb stung me. That was the end of my fishing for the day.

I always liked being near water, whether I was fishing or not. If the fish weren't biting, I just enjoyed the day, listening to the birds, looking at the lily pads, watching a turtle or a frog. In the spring of the year, I enjoyed hearing all the spring birds and listening to the frogs calling loudly.

—Susan Apps-Bodilly

My wife, Ruth, and daughter Sue fishing at our pond at Roshara, 1966.

2

Of Poles, Rods, and Lures

Pretty much every time my dad drove in to Wild Rose, he had a reason to stop at Hotz's Hardware on Main Street. If he needed a bolt or some nails or maybe a new handsaw, Hotz's had it. If he needed some paint and a new paintbrush, Hotz's had it.

The place had a special smell, a combination of all the items Dick Hotz had for sale mixed with the aroma of wood smoke from the big woodstove that stood in the back room of the store. I was especially drawn to the fishing section, where I could buy a sixteen-foot cane fishing pole for about a dollar, along with a length of heavy, green-braided fishline—guaranteed not to break—a red-and-white bobber, and some fishhooks.

Dick Hotz liked kids, and I liked him. He would take the time to help me search through the fishing equipment, and when I bought hooks with the ten cents I had in my pocket, he usually tossed in an extra hook or two. He put them in a little envelope just like the ones the Methodist church used for Sunday morning contributions.

My dad and brothers and I used cane poles for many years. According to my brother Darrel, who many years later studied botany, the poles were made from a species of bamboo, *Phyllostachus aurea*, that has the common name Fish Pole Bamboo. "The canes were about fifteen feet long and about one and half to two inches in diameter at the base and yellow in color," Darrel told me. "I learned that this species was native of Fujian and Zhejiang, China. Although the species can be grown in USDA zone 6 and 7, they probably were being imported from China clear back in the 1940s."

We got good at tossing our lines out into a lake. We learned to not stand too close to one another, as a baited hook flying through the air might catch one of us in the ear or in the sleeve of our jackets, putting a stop to fishing until the wandering hook was removed and the ear patched up.

I watched other anglers when we were fishing with our cane poles. Most of them had fishing rods of one kind or another. Fishing with a fancy fishing rod looked so much easier than flinging the line out into the lake with a cane pole. One summer I decided I wanted a fishing rod and spent hours poring over the pages of casting rods pictured in the Sears, Roebuck catalog. Pa paid me a penny a bushel for picking potatoes every fall. We had twenty acres of potatoes—that's a lot of potatoes to pick—so I was able to save a few dollars.

Finally, the next spring, I saw just the casting rod I thought I'd like and ordered it from Sears. It arrived several days later—and what a beauty it was. After I'd pushed the two pieces together, it was only about five feet long, far shorter than our cane poles. The rod came with a reel filled with thin black fishline, with a crank handle on the side. I couldn't wait to try it out, and I headed out to the yard. I quickly tied a bobber on the end of the line for a bit a weight, took hold of my rod, and gave it generous swing with my arm. The fishline shot out of the reel as the bobber sailed through the air, traveling a distance far greater than anything I could achieve with my cane pole. Soon the bobber hit the ground, but the reel kept turning and turning, tangling the line in a mess like I had never seen. I spent more than an hour untangling the line. I'd never had this kind of problem with my cane pole.

A few days later, I mentioned what had happened to my cousin Harold. Harold was a first-rate fisherman who had several casting rods.

"Tell me exactly what happened," he asked.

I explained in detail. He laughed.

"You forgot to do something important when you tossed out the line," he told me. "You've got to hold your thumb on the reel and stop it from turning when the bobber hits the water."

"Oh," I said. "I didn't know that."

I kept practicing with my casting rod—and mostly succeeded in not tangling the line as I had that first time. But I never got good at it. I switched to a spinning rod and found I could toss the line as far as I could with the casting rod. In recent years, I have become comfortable using a spinning rod with a closed reel. I use an assortment of bait with it, from earthworms to fancy lures, all with ease—and no tangles.

I have also tried fishing with a fly rod. These long, flexible rods require considerable finesse to master them. For fly fishing, you use a heavier fishline than you would on a spinning rod, wrapping it around your hand and then, while flinging the fly rod back and forth, letting a bit of line fly off your hand. Using a fly rod properly is an art form, one I can't say I have mastered.

SPINNING ROD MISHAP

When my dad was in his mid-seventies, he and his friend Robert Gast decided to try their luck fishing one warm summer afternoon on Wilson Lake, east of Wild Rose. Both fishermen were using spinning rods. Pa had two of them: one he held in his hand, and the other he tucked under his leg. Two big red-and-white bobbers floated a few feet from the boat as Pa dozed in the warm summer sun. And then it happened. As Pa later told it, "The rod tucked under my leg—it was a new one that I'd just gotten—slammed against my leg. I grabbed for the handle, but I had to drop the rod I was holding first, and I couldn't get to the new one in time. The new rod slipped over the side of the boat. I watched it sink in ten or twelve feet of water."

Any angler knows losing a rod is the worst thing that can happen. It's like leaning your deer rifle against the side of the tree and not remembering where you left it. What is there to do when your new fishing rod has disappeared? You're left to wonder how big that bluegill was that jerked your rod out of the boat and carried it down into deep water.

The two old fishermen sat for a minute or two, pondering the situation. They couldn't see the lost rod in the water. But they were intent on trying to retrieve it before they left the lake. Pa tied a lure on the line of his other rod, the kind that had multiple hooks and would sink when you left it alone on the water. He tossed the lure again and again, and then, to his surprise, he snagged the line on his submersed rod. He brought the rod up to the surface, grabbed hold of it, and started pulling on the line. The line came alive. "Something big on the other end," Pa said to his fishing buddy. He wondered how that could be, as he had been using a small, number-eight hook. The line continued to jerk, so he decided to leave it alone for a bit. Then he began pulling on the line again, piling up the fishline in the bottom of the boat. He then worked on cranking all the loose line back onto the reel. When that task was finished, he began cranking on the rod's reel, wondering what kind of giant fish was on the other end.

This time there was no tugging and pulling; the line came along slow and easy. Soon a good-sized bluegill lay flopping in the bottom of the boat. It was hooked on the lip, and it had a mass of bite marks on it. Pa figured a big northern pike had grabbed the bluegill after he'd hooked it, and then then let go when he started pulling it in. Along with having gotten his new spinning rod back and catching a nice-sized bluegill, he had a new fish tale to tell.

THE PERFECT LURE

When I was a kid fishing with a cane pole, my bait of choice was earthworms in summer and minnows in winter. We didn't use lures in those days, as they don't really work when fishing with a cane pole and bobber. I was probably in high school before I fished with a lure for the first time—and I have been searching for the perfect fishing lure ever since. By "perfect" I mean a foolproof, never-fail lure that will attract several species of fish, any time of the day. Evidence suggests such a lure does not exist.

In the 1970s, *Wheaties* cereal boxes advertised a fishing contest. "Write your unbelievable fishing story," the ad proclaimed. "Win a new motorboat!" A flashy blue boat was pictured skimming across the waves of a lake. My kids and I decided that we ought to enter the contest, as we could surely come up with an unbelievable fishing story. But as we talked about our adventures of the past several years, they didn't seem particularly unbelievable, merely ordinary stories of a guy fishing with his kids.

Then, one day we were talking fishing with a neighbor. He told us about two fellows he'd heard of who'd gotten reservations for a week at a little out-of-the way place in Manitoba, Canada. When they arrived at the lodge, they discovered the owner wasn't there. His wife said he had flown all the way to the Arctic Circle, where he'd heard the fish were biting. (Apparently you can never go too far north to catch fish!) This sounded a bit unbelievable to me, so I wrote it up and read it to the kids. They liked the story and agreed we'd surely win the boat with it. I sent it in to Wheaties, along with a box top, and promptly forgot about it. But the kids didn't forget. In a week or so, they began asking, "Dad, did you hear if we won the Wheaties boat yet?

Several weeks later, a small package arrived in the mail. In it was a basic fishing lure—a jointed minnow—and a note from General Mills saying our entry was one of the lucky winners. They didn't say who had won the boat or what other prizes had been awarded, but ours must have been toward the bottom of the list.

The next time the kids and I went fishing for bluegills, I decided to try the new lure. On my second appraisal, I decided it was a rather attractive lure, black on the top and white on the bottom, with a smear of yellow around each eye and a blotch of red under its chin. I tossed out the lure and slowly began reeling it in. I was impressed with its realistic action. I hadn't reeled it in but a few feet when a good-sized largemouth bass grabbed it. I landed the bass and tossed out the lure again. This time I landed a rock bass. After an hour had passed, I had caught four good-sized bass. Did we happen to hit a good night for bass fishing, or was this success all due to my new lure? I could hardly wait to try it again. It was a winning lure for a while—until it got caught on some brush and I lost it.

Lures are imitations of live bait used to attract fish. There are hundreds of lures available; some are used for casting (throwing the baited hook a distance and then reeling it back), and some are used for trolling (dragging the baited hook through the water as the boat moves at a consistent speed). The choices are many—jigs, crankbaits, spoons, plastic earthworms, spinners, and flies—and certain lures work best for different fish and fishing circumstances. For instance, a crankbait is a moving bait made for catching predatory species of fish under the surface. These lures are designed to appear like a moving fish or animal and allow the user to control how deep they dive into the water.[3]

Most fish prefer live bait over something artificial, but artificial lures are more convenient. You can store lures in your tackle box for any length of time and easily switch from one to another if the fish are not attracted by your first choice. Live bait, such as minnows and worms, must be cared for and kept at appropriate temperatures. Lures also can work well for waking up inactive fish. A largemouth bass might strike at a moving lure, for example, while ignoring a live minnow floating under a bobber.

Artificial lures have their downsides: they are more expensive than live bait, and they are easily lost when they get hung up on underwater weeds or brush.

Over the years, I have tried many different lures: ones that floated and ones that sank; ones that had moving parts and ones that did not; ones that looked like a minnow, ones that looked like a worm, and ones that didn't look like anything. I've learned that for most anglers, the kind of lure you use does make a big difference—as long as you're catching fish.

~ FISH TALE ~

Winning Lure

My son Jeff, who lives in Colorado, tells this story that he remembers from a family camping trip to Yellowstone National Park in 1977, when he was thirteen.

It was a cool mid-June morning, and the cutthroat trout season had just started. We stopped by a local store to get some fishing information. A man at the store said to use a small, gold, rectangular-shaped lure with red dots on it. So I bought one for each of us kids. We had to mark 16 inches on our poles, as there was a rule that we could only keep trout that were smaller than that length. The larger ones were saved for spawning and had to be thrown back.

We kids all got up early and walked the short distance from our campsite to Yellowstone Lake. It was cool and calm, and we were fishing from the shore. The first cast went out, and a large cutthroat trout immediately hit the lures. Steve and I both caught trout on our first cast! The trout were too big to keep, so we had to release them. I recall seeing one trout explode with eggs when we brought it ashore. I had never seen that before. I believe we caught two or three trout small enough to keep, and we fried them up at the campsite. It was glorious!

The mark of 16 inches is still on that fishing pole. It can never be erased, nor would I ever try to erase it.

—Jeff Apps

3

Ice Fishing in the Early Days

When I was a kid, time for fishing during the busy spring and summer months on the farm was hard to come by. But during winter, and especially during the long Christmas break from school, we had ample time for ice fishing. My dad and uncles loved ice fishing, and we boys did, too. One of our favorite spots was Mt. Morris Lake, a few miles east of Wild Rose.

My dad never let cold weather get in the way of ice fishing. In the late 1930s and early 1940s, there were no ice fishing shanties on the Wisconsin lakes we fished. To keep warm on the coldest days, we built a campfire on shore. I gathered branches, and Donald and Darrel managed to find some wispy dry grass. Soon we had a fire that would keep us comfortable, dry our hands after handling bait or fish, and toast our lunchtime sandwiches.

In those days, each fisherman was allowed to have two lines in the water at a time. Pa would chop two holes in the ice for each of our tip-ups. To cut through the ice, he used the rear axle off an old Model T, sharpened on one end by his friend Arnold Christensen, the town blacksmith. Depending on how cold it had been so far that season, the ice might be as much as a foot thick. With the holes chopped, we helped Pa set up the tip-ups, each with a little red flag that would fly up if a fish took the bait, a 2- or 3-inch shiner minnow.

The next challenge on bitterly cold days was to keep the ice holes from freezing. About every half hour, one of us would make the rounds of the ice holes and remove the ice that had begun to form, using a long-handled strainer made just for this purpose.

I don't remember the exact year that I saw the first ice fishing shanties on Mt. Morris Lake, but it was likely in the late 1940s. Sitting by our smoky campfire, I sometimes envied the folks who sat inside little ice fishing shanties with their coats hanging on a nail and a stove heating the confined structure to eighty degrees or more. Always curious, one day I stopped by one of those ice fishing shanties and chatted with its inhabitant, who told me he'd hired someone to build his. After the visit, I told Pa we should have one. Of course, we didn't have the money to have one built. I knew my dad would think of a way we might get our own shanty, without it costing an "arm and a leg," as he often said when he talked about buying something.

When we got home, we put away our ice fishing equipment, and Pa headed off to the potato cellar, a small building built into the hill just west of our chicken house. During the years that Pa raised potatoes as a cash crop, he stored the potatoes in the bottom of the potato cellar. Above that was an area where Pa stored farm machinery.

At the supper table that night, Pa said he had an idea for an ice fishing shanty. He talked about a little shack he kept in the storage area of the potato cellar. He called it a sleigh coupe. As a curious little kid, I had explored the potato cellar many times and had seen it sitting off by itself in the corner. When I asked what it had been used for, Pa explained that the coupe was put on the front of a horse-drawn bobsled and served as a shelter for the driver. When Pa raised potatoes, he harvested them in the fall and stored them in the potato cellar until late February or March. Then he loaded them on the bobsled, put the coupe on the sled, hooked up the team, and drove the load to Wild Rose, where the potato buyers and their warehouses were located.

The sleigh coupe was about six feet by six feet square and tall enough for a short person to stand in. It had two big windows in the front, with a slot under the windows for the lines to the horses. There was a little window in the back, a bench to sit on, and a small metal stove on the floor in one corner. With no more winter trips to the potato warehouses, Pa decided to convert the sleigh coupe into an ice fishing shanty. All he needed to do was to figure out how to attach runners to the bottom so we could pull it out onto the lake and fill in the slot under the front windows to keep out the cold winter winds.

With our new shanty situated on Mt. Morris Lake, no longer did we keep warm by a smoky campfire. Now we could sit in our little former sleigh coupe, keep an eye on our tip-ups out the front windows, and stay cozy warm thanks to the stove that sat in one corner. It was a bit of a tight fit when my two brothers, Pa, and I were all inside at the same time. But we made do. When a tip-up flag flew up, it was a bit of a humorous circus as the four us all tried to go out the small door at the same time, often getting stuck in the process.

Later we learned that some anglers who were fishing for bluegills and perch had a hole in the bottom of their fish shanties positioned over a hole in the ice. They could sit inside their warm shanty out of the wind and fish without wearing gloves. Their hole in the ice didn't freeze over. Unfortunately, Pa never made this modification to our sleigh coupe shanty.

As the years went by, ice fishing shanties got fancier and fancier, with more windows and more seating space. But not ours. It was forever a sleigh coupe converted into an ice fishing shanty, with no further improvement. Still, it served us well and had many stories to tell.

Our old sleigh coupe, seen here with my father, neighbor Frank Kolka, Donald and Darrel, and David Kolka, served us well as a fish shanty. Note the windup phonograph sitting on the roof. We liked to listen to records while waiting for fish to bite.

There came a date in late winter—I believe it was March 15—by which the DNR said that all ice shanties had to be removed from the lakes. It was a good rule, as otherwise shanties would end up floating or sinking into the lake as the ice melted. One year, a thaw came early and melted just enough of the lake's frozen surface so that when it froze again, our ice shanty was frozen in place. We solved the problem, sort of, by sawing off the bottom of the coupe, leaving it stuck in the ice. This marked the end of our using the old sleigh coupe as a shanty. We moved the remains of the little shack back to the farm. I don't know what became of the floor and its two runners when the ice finally melted and the lake was once again open for summer fishing. They may be on the bottom of Mt. Morris Lake still.

~ FISH TALE ~

Ice Fishing Memory

My brother Darrel shared this story of a special day on Mt. Morris Lake when he was sixteen.

We had a fishing shack that we used when it was especially cold, but this day was fairly mild, and we spent the day outside, on the ice, talking to friends and watching our tip-ups. Our neighbor boys, Dave and Jim Kolka, who shared the fishing house, were there along with our dad, my brother Don, and high school buddies Ron and John Nelson and Helen Hudziak, who owned a bar in the village of Wild Rose and was also a bartender. Helen was loved by everyone. Her verbal discourse, however, reflected her bar clientele and wasn't meant to be heard by teenage boys. Knowing this, we listened intently to hear her conversations!

About 2 p.m., my tip-up flag went up, and I ran to the fishing hole. I couldn't believe how fast the fishline spool was spinning. I waited a few seconds and then set the hook. With that, the fish seemed to take off in another direction. Gradually, I started pulling the fish in and realized it was a big one. Finally, I saw the fish and immediately called my dad to come with the gaff hook. I wondered if the fishing hole was going to be large enough and if the fishing line was strong enough. After a few attempts to get the fish lined up with the hole, my father was able to insert the gaff hook, and together we pulled the fish out onto the ice. By this time many of the fishermen in the area had come to see what was happening, and I became the celebrity of the day! This northern pike was 31 inches long and weighed just a little over ten pounds, by no means a record but a good-sized catch!

—Darrel Apps

4

Messing About in Boats (and Canoes)

I was about ten years old the first time I went fishing in a boat. Pa and my brothers and I were headed to Norwegian Lake, halfway between Wild Rose and Mt. Morris. On the way, we stopped at the Andersons' farm, where they had wooden boats for rent. Pa gave Mrs. Anderson a dollar, which allowed us to use a boat for the full day. She fetched a pair of wooden oars from a shed near the house, and soon we were driving on a trail along the edge of the Andersons' cow pasture to the boat landing, which consisted of a short wooden pier and three or four wooden boats resting on shore.

We unloaded our cane poles, our cans of worms, a pail, and the boat anchor we'd fashioned from a broken plow point and a length of old rope Pa found in the machine shed.

"Pick out a good boat," Pa said. I stood looking at the old wooden boats, which all seemed to be identical. I pointed to one. Pa flipped it over, and the four of us pushed it in the water alongside the pier. We piled in with our gear, and I noticed Pa tossed in an old empty coffee can that was lying near the boats. Then Pa fitted the oars into the oarlocks, and we were off to what he called the marl hole.

Norwegian Lake was one of many in central Wisconsin that had a marl bottom: an ancient collection of aquatic plants and animals that resulted in a material high in calcium carbonate. For many years, marl was dredged from the bottom of central Wisconsin lakes and used for fertilizer to increase the pH level of soil for alfalfa fields. The dredging left a "marl hole" twenty-five feet deep. In the heat of summer, fish migrated to the cooler water of the marl hole.

Pa said to keep looking over the side of the boat, and when I couldn't see the bottom of the lake, we'd know we had reached the marl hole. It took about fifteen minutes of rowing to get there. "I can't see the bottom," I said in an excited voice. The lake was smooth as glass. Gazing into the black waters of the dredged-out marl hole, I wondered what lived down there. Big fish, I hoped.

Pa stopped rowing and tossed the makeshift anchor into the lake so it would hit bottom just before the deep drop-off of the marl hole. We all got busy unwinding the fishline from our cane poles and adjusting our bobbers. Pa said to slip the bobber up about fifteen feet from the hook. We threaded wiggly worms onto our hooks and tossed them into the lake, wondering if Pa was right about big fish living in this deepest part of the lake.

Before my bobber even hit the lake, Donald's went under and he horsed out a bluegill the size of Pa's hand. Darrel's bobber did the same, then Pa's, and finally mine. It was like that for the next fifteen minutes. One bluegill after another, caught and dropped into the fish pail. But then something else caught my attention. I had been so busy catching fish, I hadn't noticed that my shoes were getting wet.

"Pa, I think this boat is leaking," I said.

Pa looked down and said, "Yup, expect all these old wooden boats leak. That's what that empty can is for. When the water gets a little deeper, take the can and bail out the water." He returned to looking for his bobber, which had disappeared, meaning he had another fish on.

Soon the fish pail was half full of fresh-caught bluegills. But I was distracted. "Pa, the water is coming over my shoes," I said.

I had put down my fish pole and was spending most of my time with the bailing can. And I was losing the battle. The water in the boat kept getting deeper.

"Are we gonna sink?" Darrel asked. None of us had life jackets.

"Nah, not if your brother keeps bailing," Pa said. "Keep your eye on your bobber. Look—you got another bite."

A few minutes later, with the water in the boat deeper still, Pa said, "Guess we got enough fish for one day." He pulled up the anchor and began rowing back toward the pier. "Better keep bailing," he said to me.

When we arrived at the pier, we took out our things, including the two worm cans, now nearly empty and floating in the water in the bottom of the boat. We pulled the boat up on shore and dumped out the water. We tied the cane poles on the Plymouth and put the pail of bluegills in the back seat with my brothers.

"Quite a day for fishing," Pa said. "Oh—you best not tell your ma about the leaky boat. She doesn't like to hear about such things."

My dad, brothers, and I generally fished from shore or rented a boat. My dad never owned a boat. He said they cost too much, and besides, why do you need to own one when you can rent one? One time, I pointed out that the boats we usually rented had seen better days, and most of them leaked. His response was, "Look at all the money we save by not having a boat. And with a leaky boat, there is usually a can handy to bail out the water."

After I began working and had saved a bit of money, one of the first things I wanted was a boat—one that would not leak. At a Sears store one day, I spotted a 12-foot aluminum boat. It would not leak, and flotation devices under the seats ensured that no matter what happened, it would not sink. It was light enough I could carry it on top of my car. I didn't have enough money to

Messing About in Boats (and Canoes) 33

In later years my father would join me or one of his friends for boat fishing, but he always preferred fishing from shore.

buy a boat motor, and I didn't mind rowing. For many years when people asked me what size motor I had on my boat, my answer was, "One Apps-power."

I have that boat to this day. Many years after I purchased it, I bought a used 4-horsepower motor from one of my dad's friends. I used it a few times but soon decided that rowing a boat was much more dependable than this old, close-to-worn-out motor. The 4-horsepower motor has hung in the shed at my farm for many years. The boat, on the other hand, has served me well for decades.

One spring shortly after I began teaching at the University of Wisconsin in Madison, the chair of my department, Walt Bjoraker, asked if I'd like to go along with him and his boys on a weekend fishing trip in northern Wisconsin.

"Sure," I replied. I almost always said yes to an opportunity to go fishing. When we arrived at the Bjorakers' cottage, I noticed there was no boat tied to the pier, just two canoes learning against the cabin.

The following morning, Walt said, "Well, are you ready for some good fishing?"

I said I was, but I wondered how we would do it. I quickly had my answer.

Walt said, "Gordie and I will take one canoe, you and Gary take the other."

"Okay," I answered. I didn't mention that I had never been in a canoe. My dad's words rang in my head, "Stay out of canoes, they ain't safe. They tip over easy."

Soon I was sitting in the front end of a 17-foot Grumman aluminum canoe, more than a little concerned about what I was getting myself into. "Gordie is good with a canoe," Walt had said. I quickly discovered that he was, as we paddled away from the pier out into the lake to where Walt had said we'd likely catch fish. I also learned that paddling a canoe is far easier than rowing a boat. We moved quickly through the water with Gordie paddling and steering in the back and me paddling in the front. I soon got over my fear that the canoe was about to tip over any minute as we sliced through the water.

We arrived at our designated fishing spot, and I hung a spinner on my line and tossed it close to a group of pond lilies. I hadn't cranked the spinner back three feet when I got a strike and landed a nice smallmouth bass. I discovered it was just as easy to land a big fish in a canoe as it was in the 12-foot aluminum boat.

I knew a canoe must join my aluminum boat, and soon I had acquired one. Of course, the canoe was considerably lighter than my boat, and it became my travel partner for the many years that I wilderness camped and fished in the Boundary Waters of northern Minnesota.

The Grumman canoe I bought weighed about eighty pounds. As the years passed, my son Steve, who did the portaging, said the Grumman canoe seemed to be getting heavier every year. We began looking for a lighter canoe and soon found a 17-foot

Messing About in Boats (and Canoes)

Canoeing in the Boundary Waters in my handy Wenonah.

Wenonah canoe that weighed about fifty-five pounds yet had the carrying capacity of our old Grumman. We now have two canoes in our shed, along with the aluminum boat.

When I reached my late seventies and getting in and out of a boat or canoe became a challenge, my brother Don and I bought a used pontoon boat, complete with a finicky motor. By finicky, I mean that on more than one occasion we would be a considerable distance from the boat landing when the motor would not start. We'd have to paddle the boat, with considerable difficulty, back to the landing. One time we even got a tow from another fisherman who saw us paddling the big pontoon boat with two little paddles. But a finicky boat that gets us out on the water is surely better than no boat at all.

Fishing Equipment Basics

FOR WARM-WEATHER FISHING

Casting rod: A fishing rod that includes a reel mounted on the top, near the handle; the fishline is wound on the reel and moves through guides on the rod. The guides on a casting rod face upward, intended to prevent the line from tangling during casting. The angler tosses the baited hook (or lure) over the water and then uses a button or lever to release the line where he or she wants the bait to drop.

With my tackle box and a couple of rods in hand, I'm ready to head to the lake for an afternoon of fishing in this photo from 1972.

Fishing Equipment Basics

Fly rod: A specialized rod, usually thinner, longer, and lighter than a casting rod, used for flyfishing. The fishline is kept in a reel, and the angler casts it repeatedly back and forth to build momentum and to fool the fish into thinking an insect is landing on the water. Bamboo is the favored material for fly rods.

Landing net: A handled net used to bring a hooked fish in from the water.

Leader: A length of line, often monofilament but sometimes braided wire, used to connect the fishing lure to the main line.

Reel: A device with a crank handle that fastens to a fishing rod and holds the fishline.

Spinning rod: A rod designed to be used with a spinning reel and a bail to control the movement of the fishline. Spinning rods are generally easier to use than casting rods, making them great for beginners.

Tackle: Equipment used for fishing.

Tackle box: A handled box in which fishing tackle is stored.

FOR ICE FISHING

Fish shanty: A small enclosed structure that is pulled onto lake ice and typically left for the winter season. A place, when ice fishing, to stay warm as you wait for fish to bite.

Fish shelter: A tentlike structure that provides a shield from the weather. It is moved on and off the lake with the anglers.

Gaff hook: A large hook attached to a handle and used to pull a large fish from the ice fishing hole after it has been hooked.

Ice auger: A large screw used to cut holes in the ice. May be gasoline or hand powered.

Ice chisel: A steel rod sharpened on one end and used to cut holes in the ice.

Ice strainer: A metal scoop with a handle used to remove ice chips from a recently cut ice hole. Also used to remove re-forming ice from fish holes on days that are well below freezing.

Jig pole: A short fishing pole used by an ice fisher who is fishing for panfish.

Sinker: A weight fastened to a fishline a few inches above the hook. The weight takes the fishline and bait to the angler's desired depth.

Tip-up: A device used to suspend live bait at a given depth through a hole cut in the ice. Tip-ups allow ice fishers to have multiple lines below the ice. When a fish bites, a flag flies up, indicating a fish is hooked.

5

Kids' First Fishing Adventures

One of my first fishing trips with our kids was also one of our first camping trips. Sue was four, Steve was three, and Jeff was two. Ruth and I selected a campground near Pardeeville—close enough to Madison that if something went wrong, we would be only an hour or so away from home. The kids were excited, especially when I suggested that we might also do some fishing in the small pond at the campground. They had never been fishing or camping.

We set up our old umbrella tent, which had seen better days. All the while the boys kept asking when we were going fishing. "Soon," I said, as I laid out the sleeping bags and helped Ruth with the camp stove and the cooking gear. Sue said she wanted to stay at the campsite and help Mommy.

I had purchased a little yellow plastic fishing rod for each of the kids, and with fishing poles in hand, the boys and I soon were off to the campground's little pond. "What are we gonna catch?" Jeff asked.

"I don't know," I said. "When you are fishing, you never know what you'll catch."

"Why not?" Steve asked.

I didn't have a good answer for him, because I have always been surprised at what kind of fish I'm able to pull from the water.

I baited an earthworm for each of the boys and helped them toss their lines out into the pond. Two little red-and-white bobbers danced on the ripples kicked up by a slight breeze. A minute went by, then another.

"When are the fish gonna bite?" Jeff asked, as he reeled in his line and tried to toss it out into the pond again. I helped him and handed the fishing pole back to him. I could see that he was getting impatient. Meanwhile, Steve stood hold-

Steve and Jeff fishing at Roshara in 1972.

ing his pole as I had taught him, not saying anything, just concentrating on the bobber floating a few feet in front of him.

Then I heard a loud splash. I turned to see that Jeff had given up fishing and tossed his fishing rod into the pond. "No dumb fish in this pond," he said and stomped back to our campsite, where his mother and sister were preparing supper. With a long stick, I was able to retrieve his fish pole from where it floated a few feet off shore. So much for Jeff's first fishing experience.

As the kids got older, Steve continued as a patient angler, while Jeff had trouble waiting for something to happen. Sue's interest in fishing grew, too, along with her love of being out in nature. We all continued fishing together as the kids were growing up, often joined by Ruth, who knew fishing was a great way to get the kids outside and learn the value of patience.

About a year after that less-than-perfect first fishing adventure, Ruth, the kids, and I were visiting my parents at their home farm near Wild Rose. My dad suggested we go fishing at Chain O' Lake, about a mile and half away. With a goodly number of bluegills—perfect for kids just becoming acquainted with fishing—it was a good place for a grandpa, three little kids, and their parents to fish. Pa still kept several cane poles tucked up on the eaves of the corn crib, and I retrieved three shorter ones for the kids along with three 16-footers for us adults.

At the lake, I baited the kids' hooks and helped them toss their lines into the water. And then we waited. Waiting for a fish to bite is no fun for little ones, as I had learned from our experience in Pardeeville. It was a glorious Sunday morning, and at first no one cared that the bobbers weren't bobbing. But soon, Steve said, "When you are fishing, shouldn't you be catching fish?" Wise words from a four-year-old. The youngsters' mother, always a bit skeptical about these fishing outings no matter that three generations were involved, soon chimed in: "Looks like another 'fish aren't biting' day."

My dad scratched his head and said, "I can't understand it. The fish always bite here. They're not very big, but they always bite." He had no more than said it when Steve's bobber dipped beneath the surface and he landed a sunfish the size of a silver dollar. Everyone was happy now, including Grandpa, who had been proven right that "the fish always bite here."

A few minutes later, Ruth and Susie each hooked a miniature sunfish. Then it was quiet again. Ruth was dozing in the warm sun when Susie's bobber went skimming out toward the middle of the lake. After a lot of splashing, giggling, and little-girl screams, Susie landed a fair-sized sunfish with Ruth's help—and took the prize for the largest fish caught that day.

While Ruth and Susie gloated over their biggest-fish honor, Steve and Grandpa were taking in one little sunfish after another. Steve took the honors for most fish caught, with five. A bit later, Grandpa landed a six-inch bullhead and tied it to Jeff's line. He had a fish now, too.

The old fishing hole had paid off again. As soon as the youngsters were back at Grandma and Grandpa's house, they put the fish in a pail of water and watched them. I'll bet they were also swapping fish stories. You can't start telling fish tales too young.

Once the kids had a few fishing adventures under their belts, they were ready for more. Now you could mention fishing at our house, and the boys, especially, were immediately wide-eyed and excited.

One Friday evening at the supper table, I casually mentioned that tomorrow might be a good day for fishing. At five-thirty the following morning, I woke to four-year-old Steve standing next to our bed, shaking my arm. "Daddy, I thought we were going fishing today," he said.

Five-year-old Sue in 1967.

After a rapidly eaten breakfast, the boys and I trekked out to the garden in search of earthworms. Jeff, then three, thought looking for worms was almost as much fun as fishing. He was down on all fours, inspecting each shovelful of soil that I turned. As soon as he spotted a worm, he put it in the middle of his little hand and watched it wiggle. After some giggling and lost worms, we had assembled enough bait and were off to the lake.

Having learned that little boys' patience is quite short, I kept our fishing excursions at the time to a couple of hours. On this day, we chose a nearby lake where the boys could fish from shore and have a fair chance of hooking a bluegill or sunfish.

Some words of caution when fishing with two little boys: don't seat them too close together, or you'll spend valuable fishing time untangling lines, bobbers, hooks, and worms. They enjoy a certain amount of, "I can get my bobber farther out in the lake than you can," so be ready to duck when a misdirected gob of worms flies over your head.

Fishing with two little boys is also a time when you find yourself answering a lot of questions like "What's that, Daddy?" and "Why does a fish [or bird or other creature] do that?" and many more. After several mallard ducks swam near us, the boys wanted to know all about "birds that float on water." Later, we spotted a mallard's nest on shore with six eggs in it. The boys were fascinated and thought the eggs should be in a refrigerator.

Another popular question: "Why are all these bugs swishing around my head?"

I never had an answer for that one, as flies were usually swishing around my head as well and I couldn't say exactly why.

Of course, the most common question was (and still is), "How come the fish aren't biting?" I've been asking the same question for many years, and nobody has given me a straight answer yet. One time while I stood there scratching my head, trying to come up with a reasonable answer, like the water was too cold or the worm wasn't wiggling enough, Jeff piped up with, "I know why the fish don't bite, Daddy. We're fishing at the wrong place. Let's go to Grandpa Apps's house. We always catch fish on the lake there."

We went home without any fish that morning and soon were making plans to drive the little fishermen to Grandpa's house at Wild Rose, where "the fish always bite."

~ FISH TALE ~

Not Only Fish Get Hooked

Take three kids, three spinning rods, a dozen nightcrawlers, and other assorted fishing do-dads, put them all in a boat—and this is what can happen.

When the kids were eleven, ten, and nine, I took them out fishing on Lake George in Oneida County. The boys shared the back seat of the boat. "We want to troll while you row, Dad," they said. At this age, they also wanted to be as far from their sister as they could get.

I rowed past a weed bed, the boys anticipating a northern biting any minute. We'd heard that someone had caught a nice-sized northern in this spot. But on this evening, there was no action. The only sound was the swish of the oars as they cut into the smooth water and created little whirlpools.

I rowed toward a place where we had previously caught perch. The sun was low on the horizon, and it would be dark in a half hour or so. When he couldn't catch a perch, Jeff switched to one of his artificial lures and began casting it toward the nearby weed bed. At the same time, my red-and-white bobber began skidding a few inches and then sank beneath the surface.

"Dad, you've got one," Sue yelled. I set the hook and began cranking on my reel. "Get the net ready," I yelled to Steve. It felt like a bass, but I couldn't be sure. Steve reached for the net just as Jeff yelled something about his leg.

I brought the fish near the boat; it wasn't as large as I thought, but to be sure I would land it, I asked Steve to net it. Steve dipped the net into the water but missed netting the fish by a foot. Jeff was yelling, "My leg, my leg!"

"What's the matter, Steve?" I asked. He tried again and missed once more. And Jeff kept yelling that his leg was hurting. Steve and I finally got the fish, a ten-inch crappie, into the boat. Now I had to find out what was happening on the back seat of the boat. One glance and I saw the problem. Jeff had somehow gotten his lure caught in a pant leg. When I had asked Steve for the net, his jacket sleeve got caught by the same lure. When Steve moved, the lure began digging into Jeff's leg.

Sue thought it was all quite funny. The boys had her believing that they were experts in this business of fishing. Now she knew the truth.

6

Bullheads and Bluegills

To some people, a bullhead is a homely black fish in a category one notch above carp. To our three kids, who were just becoming acquainted with fishing, there was no finer fish than a bullhead. They formed this opinion because we had many bullheads in the pond at our farm, Roshara, and they would bite almost any time of the day.

One early evening in July 1968, my dad and I trekked down to the pond with the kids, then ages six, five, and four. The kids were eager to go fishing. I started threading an earthworm onto each youngster's hook. Jeff immediately tossed his baited line into the water. While I was baiting up Steve's hook, Sue began yelling "Jeff, Jeff, you've got a bite!"

Not quite remembering what he was supposed to do when a bobber went under, Jeff just stared as it appeared and disappeared. I got to him and helped him pull a well-hooked bullhead from the water. He was a very proud little boy. Luckily, I had remembered to bring leather gloves, to avoid being stung by the sharp whiskers characteristic of bullheads. I put another worm on Jeff's hook, and his line was soon back in the water. By the time I had Steve's line baited and in the water, Jeff had another fish, which he pulled in by himself. He was content to watch his little

Jeff, Steve, and my dad at the Roshara pond in 1967.

bullhead flopping around while I got Sue's line ready. It turned out to be one of the busiest fishing outings I had ever been a part of. Thankfully, Grandpa was there to help take fish off hooks and thread worms onto hooks. Inside of an hour, Sue, Steve, and Jeff yanked, dragged, pulled, and otherwise got out of the pond forty-five bullheads; the biggest was about six inches long. Some would fall off the hook as soon as they came out of the pond. We tossed them all in a pail half filled with water.

Steve held his fish pole in one hand and my trout landing net in the other. When a bullhead would fall off the hook, land on the bank, and start tumbling back toward the pond, he clamped the net over the fish, quite proud of his save. After about fifteen such saved bullheads, a frog jumped in front of Steve. He quickly decided a frog would be more of a challenge than the bullheads flopping on shore, so, with his bobber bobbing with another bite, he scurried along the shore, trying to drop the net over a frog.

Finally, after three or four misses, he was successful. He ran to me, boasting, "Look, Dad, I got a frog!" This is quite an achievement, especially if you've never caught one before. After some persuasion, I convinced him to let the frog go and get back to his fish pole. His bobber had long since sunk out of sight. He pulled in one more bullhead to add to the pail.

As it was getting dark, I convinced the kids that we should toss the pail of little bullheads back in the pond and return to the cabin. I couldn't wait to hear the fish stories they had for their mother. Grandpa Apps had a big smile on his face, likely remembering the times when my brothers and I were little kids full of fish stories.

When the kids were little, we usually concentrated on catching bluegills as well as bullheads. Bluegills can reach as long as 12 inches, but the ones we caught usually ranged from tiny (not much larger than a silver dollar) to the size of a man's hand. They were fun to catch, as they usually put up a good tugging battle, and they were good to eat, especially soon after they were caught. The kids preferred bluegills because they liked the action the little fish offered.

I recall a time when the kids were young and we got up early and drove to Norwegian Lake so we'd be there when the bluegills were feeding. My dad had taught me about bluegill beds, where the fish clear a place on the bottom of the lake to lay their eggs and hatch their little ones. Finding bluegills on their bed was our goal that morning. The challenge was finding the bed and then anchoring the boat in the right spot—close enough so a worm-baited hook could be dropped over a bluegill nest and far enough away to avoid scaring the fish. The beds are usually in water only two or three feet deep, which meant rowing along the shore and gazing over the side until we spotted the beds. The kids didn't like all this time spent searching; they wanted to fish. So, as I slowly rowed, they tossed out their baited hooks, sometimes close to shore and sometimes in deeper water. They caught bluegills, too. Whenever one of them caught a fish, the other one tossed his line in the same spot and the lines tangled—and guess who had to stop rowing and untangle the mess of monofilament line?

"Let me find the beds, then we'll anchor and we all can fish," I said.

"Why do we need to find a fish bed when the fish are bitin' right here?" Steve asked.

I tried to describe a bluegill bed, but it was difficult to answer Steve's question about why the fish would bite any better if we found one. Finally, I found some beds and slipped the anchor over the side of the boat.

"Now we'll catch some of the big ones I've been telling you about," I said as I baited my hook and tossed out my line. The big bobber rode the waves without quivering. There were no fish chasing my worm-baited hook.

"Let's move to where we were before," Steve said. "The fish are all out of bed."

I pulled up the anchor and mentally crossed off the "foolproof" theory that to catch bluegills in the spring of the year, you look for them on their beds.

Wisconsin's Oldest Fish

I remember visiting the Wild Rose Fish Hatchery with my dad and mom when I was three or four years old. Often when relatives from Wisconsin Rapids or Milwaukee came to our farm, we took them to the fish hatchery. I found the place fascinating, with hundreds of trout swimming in long concrete ponds. And I was amazed when I first spotted a fish many times bigger than the largest trout. Each pond appeared to have at least one of these long, black fish.

"Pa, what kind of fish are those?" I pointed to one of them.

"Those are sturgeon," Pa answered. "They help keep the ponds clean."

Years later, I learned that sturgeon are our oldest fish. Scientists have determined, using fossil records, that sturgeon have been on earth at least 150 million years. Dinosaurs have disappeared, glaciers have formed and melted, lakes and rivers have experienced dramatic changes, yet through all of that, the sturgeon has survived.

Sturgeons have an unusual lifecycle. They can live for more than a hundred years. And they keep growing as they age. Females do not spawn until they are at least twenty years old. During the time that sturgeons spawn in Wisconsin, usually between April 15 and May 5, they swim upstream into the several streams and rivers in the Winnebago River system, a network of waterways that includes Lake Winnebago and the Fox, Wolf, and Embarass Rivers. Starting in the spring of 1988, volunteers have been enlisted to protect these huge fish from poachers and illegal fishing during spawning. Volunteers guard active spawning sites twenty-four hours a day.

The Lake Winnebago system has one of the largest lake sturgeon populations in North America. It is also home to a unique winter spearing fishery, which began in 1931. There are only two locations in North American where sturgeon can be speared; the other is Black Lake in Michigan.[4]

Annual spearfishing takes place on the Winnebago system, as well as on Lakes Butte des Mortes, Winneconne, and Poygan. Special spear fishing permits must be obtained from the Wisconsin Department of Natural Resources, and the minimum spearing age is twelve.

The record sturgeon speared in the Lake Winnebago system weighed 212.2 pounds and was speared in 2010. The second largest was speared in 2004 and weighed 188 pounds.

Sturgeon can also be fished with rod and reel. The record sturgeon for rod and reel fishing is 170 pounds, 10 ounces, and 79 inches long. It was caught in Yellow Lake (Burnett County) in 1979.[5]

7

Opening Day

When I was growing up, opening day of fishing season ranked right up there with Christmas, Thanksgiving, the Fourth of July, and the opening day of deer-hunting season in importance. No weddings, funerals, birthday parties, or other activities were planned for the fishing or hunting opener—not unless you didn't want anyone to come. Opening day fish stories are legend, shared again and again and usually embellished a bit with each telling.

Fishing seasons in Wisconsin are regulated by the Department of Natural Resources. The first Saturday in May is the traditional opening day. Special seasons and restrictions exist for certain fish species. For example, the open season for Wisconsin's northern muskie zone in 2024 was May 25–December 31; the southern muskie zone season was May 4–December 31.

OPENING DAY 1972

On opening day of fishing season in 1972, the kids were ten, nine, and eight. You've never seen sadder faces than theirs that chilly May morning. After weeks of planning, dreaming, and discussing what fish we might catch and reminiscing about what we had caught in previous years, this opening day Saturday saw raindrops drumming on the cabin windows.

Opening Day

Sid Boyum's opening day drawing from May 9, 1969. FRIENDS OF SID BOYUM, COURTESY OF THE WISCONSIN HISTORICAL SOCIETY. WHI IMAGE ID 123043

"We're still going fishing, aren't we, Dad?" they asked. I assured them we were—but not until the rain stopped.

"How long's the rain gonna last?" Jeff asked. I reminded him that the weather person on the Waupaca radio station had said there was a 70 percent chance of rain for the entire day.

But after lunch, the rain let up. We quickly loaded our aluminum boat on the car, tossed the fishing gear in the back, and drove to Mt. Morris Lake.

"Let's go to the same spot where we caught that big northern pike last winter," Steve said. "I wanna hook another one just like it."

I rowed the boat from the public landing to where Steve remembered he had caught the 25-inch northern. He snapped an imitation minnow onto his spinning rod line and tossed it toward some lily pads. Nothing happened as he reeled in his line.

Jeff tried the same type of lure and succeeded in catching my shirt so securely I had to take off the shirt and work for fifteen minutes to remove the hooks. Steve continued working his silver minnow over the area where he thought the big ones were.

"Think I'm gonna switch to worms," he said.

I continued fishing with a jointed artificial minnow and hooked a largemouth bass, 13 or 14 inches long. It fought like the fish do in the sporting magazines. It jumped out of the water and shook its head. Then it dashed toward some lily pads before I finally reeled it close enough to the boat for the net.

Now the bluegills began biting. Nearly every cast brought in a nice-sized fish. Then, on one of Jeff's casts, his hook snagged my orange cap and snapped it from my head. It flew several yards out over the lake and fell with a splash. Even I laughed as Jeff reeled in my deer hunting bonnet.

About that time, Jeff said he had to go the bathroom. A bathroom was a good five minutes of rowing away, so I said I would try for the little woods that came down to the lake.

"Make it snappy," my young companion suggested. My first attempt at landing the boat failed. It got caught in the mud and I had to pole the boat free. The second time we made it to shore.

The problem was almost solved for the little fisherman, but not quite. As he tried to leave the boat, one of his fishhooks got caught in his sock. Quickly, I yanked the hook out of his sock, and in a few minutes we were fishing again. It was a good day. Twenty bluegills and one bass—and a chance to get acquainted again with summer fishing after too many months of waiting.

OPENING DAY WITH ARNOLD

Ruth's sister Pearl and her husband, Arnold, lived on the west side of the state, in the coulee region north of La Crosse. My brother-in-law was a good fisherman—in his words. He liked to fish the Mississippi and the Black River. On one occasion in the 1980s, Arnold and Pearl came to spend a couple days with us at Roshara, arriving on the day before opening day of fishing season. Arnold said to me, "You always brag about these central Wisconsin trout. Show me where I can catch some."

I suggested we get up at dawn and drive to Willow Creek, east of Wild Rose. At five thirty, the alarm clanged. It was still dark in the cabin. Heavy, dark clouds had moved in during the night, and a few sprinkles of rain splattered on the cabin windows.

"Looks like we're gonna face a rainy morning," I said. "You wanna call off fishing?"

"You don't get out of it that easy—a little rain isn't gonna keep me from checking on those famous central Wisconsin trout," came his reply.

The rain held off as we parked the car and walked toward the creek.

"Where's the path?" Arnold asked.

"There's no path. Just walk south until you get to the creek. Look for a hole under a bank, or where the creek turns. That's where you'll find a trout waiting for your bait."

"I know how to find the holes, but how do I find the creek?" he asked.

I told him to keep walking and he'd find the creek. We separated.

I wound my way through the tangle of dogwood and wild grapes and finally found the little stream, clear and gurgling quietly through the vegetation that hung heavily over each bank.

In back of me and to the right, I heard the brush cracking and snapping as Arnold pushed through the tangled vegetation.

"Jerry, where'd you go?" I heard him yell.

"Over here," I answered.

"I'm stuck in this blamed brush and don't see any creek. You sure there's one here?" he yelled.

"Walk toward me—but watch out you don't fall in a spring hole," I cautioned.

Just then I heard a splash and several unprintable words about Willow Creek.

"I'm gonna back out of here and start over again," Arnold said. Then I didn't hear him anymore. I assumed he found the creek and all was well. I worked along the stream, trying all the holes, but with no luck. Then I came to a fence and a break in the heavy undergrowth where cows had been coming to the creek for water. There I saw Arnold sitting on the bank.

"How they biting?" I asked.

"Lousy," he answered, staring at the water. "Nothin' at all. Not a thing. 'Course, you can't expect too much without a hook. Caught my hook on a limb a while back and lost it. So, I'm just sitting here thinking about all the fish you were probably catching."

It began raining a little harder. "Guess we'll have to quit," I suggested. "No sense getting wet for a few fish." Arnold hadn't brought a rain coat.

"Sure wish it hadn't rained," I said. "We'd have gotten our limits for sure. We just needed a little more time." He just shook his head.

PESHTIGO RIVER OPENING DAY

Early May in northern Wisconsin is totally unpredictable. One day it's eighty degrees and spring, and the next it's forty degrees with an occasional snowflake in the air. It was one of the warm days when we arrived at our fishing camp on the banks of the ruggedly beautiful Peshtigo River. Trees, their buds straining to burst open, lined the edges of the river. Where we camped, the Peshtigo makes its way through Marinette County forestland. Bloodroot was in bloom, soft white, eight- to ten-petaled flowers contrasting with the green of the plant's leaves and the dull brown of the dead grass where spring growth wasn't yet evident. Birds were singing everywhere, robins, catbirds, and many others

I couldn't identify. Mallards floated on the river and lifted into the air when we approached. Walking in the woods along the river, I could sense new life in the air as spring slowly crawled out from its brown bed and stretched awake.

For many years, I returned to the Peshtigo each spring for opening day of trout season. On this occasion, the three fishermen accompanying me were new to fishing and to camping. At this time of year, the river is usually high, straining to crawl out of its channel and spill into the woods, but not this year. "Didn't have our usual snow cover," the park ranger told us. "Haven't had much rain this spring, either."

So the river was low and clear, making it difficult to fish. In previous years we had caught fish out in the center of the river, where the current was strong and steady. But not this year. Swimming in the relatively clear water, a rainbow trout or a German brown could spot an angler from far away. Few of us caught fish on this opening day, except those anglers who searched out the deep holes, around a bend in the river, near large rocks, and next to trees that had fallen into the water. The few fish we did catch were above average length, not like the 6- and 8-inch fish we often caught in the put-and-take fish streams in the southern part of the state.

That evening, we sat around the campfire listening to the popping of pine wood and watching the flames dance in the darkness. And we shared a few fish stories. Even though the day had been more successful for the fish than for the fishermen, it had been glorious, a chance to soak up the outdoors and recharge human batteries.

~ FISH TALE ~

Opening Day with Pa

Donald remembers this opening day adventure on the Wild Rose millpond with our dad.

In the early days, fishing season opened at midnight. The fish hatchery would stock the millpond, sometimes with big female trout that were no longer useful for egg production. Between 9 p.m. and midnight, a bunch of fishermen would gather on the shore of the millpond, drinking and partying. The moment the season opened at midnight, they'd begin tossing lines in the water—tangling their lines and sometimes getting in fights.

On one opening day with Pa, boats were everywhere on the millpond. Many were too close to each other. One guy in a boat kept crossing Pa's line. The second or third time he did it, tangling his line with Pa's, Pa yelled, "You do that again, I'm coming over to your boat and drown you." Pa was probably seventy-five years old at that time!

—Donald Apps

8

Fishing with Grandpa Apps

"Which lake we going to this time?" Steve asked when we arrived at my parents' farm. It was a pleasant January day, a good day for ice fishing. Steve and Jeff were looking forward to another fishing outing with their grandfather.

"Thought we'd try Round Lake," my dad answered. "I've been over there a couple times this week. Hooked a couple of northerns that weighed over 6 pounds and got a mess of bluegills, too."

We stopped at Norm's bait shop in Wild Rose and bought a supply of waxworms. Earlier, Grandpa had checked to make sure he had enough minnows for another day on the ice. We drove a few miles east of Wild Rose to Round Lake and parked the car. Grandpa, the kids, and I walked along the winding trail through the woods to the lake and hiked another short distance along the lake to the spot where my dad had been catching fish. I spotted a few anglers across the lake, but on our side, there was no one else. Quickly, I chopped holes in the ice and set up the tip-ups, carefully checking the line depth to be sure that the minnows would be floating a few feet from the lake's bottom. Then I chopped holes for the jig poles that we'd use for panfish, such as bluegills and sunfish.

Sue and Steve ice fishing with jig poles in the mid-1960s.

Grandpa and the boys unstrung the jig poles and threaded waxworms on the little hooks. "Keep jigging it up and down," Grandpa told the boys as they stared into the gray-black water that came to the tops of the fish holes in the ice. "Bluegills need some encouragement in the winter," he reminded us. "They don't move around as fast in winter as they do in summer."

Sue already knew how to use a jig pole and didn't even glance at her brothers to see how they were doing.

I kept my eye on the tip-ups, watching for one of the flags to fly up announcing someone had a northern taking their bait. An hour passed. Then another. Steve, Jeff, Sue, and their grandpa were hooking bluegills, one after the other. The fish weren't large, but the boys were having fun catching them.

"What's the matter, Dad?" Jeff asked me. "Your tip-up hasn't moved since you set it up." "I'm sure a northern will bite eventually," I said, but I didn't really know. Fish have their own clock.

While we were eating lunch, one of the tip-up flags snapped up. I ran to it, anticipating a 5-pound or bigger northern at the end of the line. But all I found was a very excited minnow on my line.

After lunch, the bluegills quit biting. The kids' patience soon wore thin, and they said they were cold. I laid out a fox and geese game in the snow on the ice, a game I had played in winter at our one-room country school. It mostly consisted of lots of running. We played for a while, until the kids had warmed up, and then they went back to bluegill fishing. I went back to staring at the inactive tip-ups.

Then the bluegills were biting again, and the children and their grandpa were once again having fun, but the tip-ups remained motionless. It was almost dark when we wound our way back up the crooked trail in the snow to the car. The kids boasted about all the fish they had caught. I wondered if we might find another lake where the northern pike would bite.

~ FISH TALE ~

"It's a Pole Bender!"

Here is a story Jeff recalls about fishing with his grandfather.

As kids, we could never swear around Mom or Dad. If we did, there were consequences that made sure that we would not repeat this action. But when we fished with our Grandpa Apps, the rules were different. He would swear at will, and we enjoyed it immensely. When he caught a fish big enough to bend his pole, he would say something like, "This fish is a real pole bender!" But if the fish got away, a series of words that we could not say or repeat came out of his mouth. He would say those words with a slight smile and a twinkle in his eye. Catching fish was not the goal for me, it was seeing my grandfather as who he really was: a child at heart who just wanted to enjoy the time with his grandkids and make them smile!

—Jeff Apps

The Language of Fishing

Folks who fish have their own language and use it regularly among themselves. The words and phrases can be a mystery to someone unfamiliar with fishing.

GENERAL TERMS

Angler: Someone who fishes, whether male or female, young or old.

Bait: Something placed on a fishhook to attract a fish. Can refer to live or artificial bait.

Barb: A sharp part of a fishhook, near the point, that prevents the hook from falling out of the fish's mouth.

Barbless hook: A hook without barbs, used for "catch and release" fishing.

Bobber: A small hollow ball that floats, often red and white and made of plastic, attached to fishline and used to suspend bait at a specific depth.

Cane pole: A fishing pole made of bamboo, usually ten feet or longer. Usually does not include a reel.

Fish fry: The tasty fried results of successful fishing.

Fish story: A tale about fishing that tends to be embellished each time it is told.

Gone fishing: Self-explanatory.

Lunker: Used to describe a big fish, usually weighing ten pounds or more (most frequently applied to northern pike, walleye, or muskellunge).

Panfish: Fish such as bluegills and sunfish that, when cleaned, easily fit into a frying pan.

HEARD WHILE FISHING IN SUMMER

Any action?: "Are you getting any bites?"

Cast: Swinging a fish pole and releasing the line, sending the bait or lure flying out over the water.

Catch and release: Releasing a live fish back into the water after catching it.

For this opening day drawing for 1971, artist Sid Boyum included this caption: "For fishing fever, there's just one cure: catch a lunker on your favorite lure." FRIENDS OF SID BOYUM, COURTESY OF THE WISCONSIN HISTORICAL SOCIETY. WHI IMAGE ID 123045

Fish aren't biting: Obvious. Bobbers remain stationary.

Fish bed: A small round structure made by fish on the bottom of a lake, often near shore. A place where fish such as bluegills spawn.

Fly fishing: A type of fishing in which the weight of the line is used for casting and artificial lures called flies are used as bait.

Got a big one on: You've hooked a large fish.

Got a bite: A fish has taken your bait and may or may not be hooked.

Got a nibble: You may have a bite—too soon to tell.

Got skunked: Caught nothing.

It's a keeper: "That's a good-sized fish." Meets minimum size length to keep the catch as allowed by local laws.

Pole bender: A fish large enough to bend your fish pole.

Strike: When a fish bites a lure or a bait.

Threw the hook: A fish somehow avoided being hooked after you thought you had a bite.

HEARD WHILE FISHING IN WINTER

Got one on: You've got a bite.

Grab the gaff hook: A cry made when the ice fishing angler realizes the fish is larger than expected and requires the help of another person to pull it from the ice fishing hole.

How deep's your line?: Question asked of a successful angler.

How much ice?: Question raised upon arriving on a lake to inquire how thick the ice is. Four inches or thicker is usually thick enough to avoid falling through when walking on the ice.

Look out for open water: Most lakes have rivers and streams running in and out of them. Avoid these areas, as the ice is thin to nonexistent in those spots.

Tip-up!: A loud announcement made when a tip-up flag flies up.

Too big for the hole: A problem encountered when a lunker is on the line and the hole was chopped for an average-sized fish.

9

Fishing Weather

My dad often used this expression when we were considering going fishing: "Just remember, when the wind is from the south, it blows the bait right into the fish's mouth. Wind from the west, and the fish bite the best. Wind from the east, the fish bite the least." Surprisingly, he had nothing to say about a north wind. I thought such sayings had little scientific merit, but I have since learned that wind direction can make a difference in fishing success.

No matter what direction it comes from, wind creates waves on a lake. A strong wind can also increase the turbidity of the water, making it difficult for the fish to see the bait. Wind accompanied by rain generally makes the water even more turbid. Bright-colored, fast-action lures work well in this situation.

I remember a Saturday when my dad and I went fishing on Gilbert Lake, north of Wild Rose. We'd fished there several times and almost always caught fish. A bit of a westerly breeze was blowing. In those days I was still relying on my 12-foot aluminum boat, which I could carry on the top of my car. I didn't have a motor and depended on rowing to power the boat.

When we arrived at the boat landing on the east side of the lake, I quickly noticed that what I had considered a breeze when

68 Lunkers, Keepers, and Ones that Got Away

Artist Sid Boyum called this drawing of fishermen in blizzard conditions "The Die Hards." (The boat is named *Sob*. Or is it *S.O.B.*?) FRIENDS OF SID BOYUM, COURTESY OF THE WISCONSIN HISTORICAL SOCIETY. WHI IMAGE ID 125546

we left Pa's place was now a stiff wind out of the west, creating substantial waves on 139-acre Gilbert Lake.

"Lake looks a little rough," I said as I got out of the car.

"It'll be fine if you row to the west side. It's mostly out of the wind," Pa replied.

We unloaded the boat from the car and put it in the water. I once more looked across the lake and noticed waves a couple feet high, at times higher.

"Doesn't look too good," I said.

"It'll be fine once we get going. With a west wind, it's a good day for fishing," Pa said.

We put our fishing gear in the boat, climbed in, and pushed off from the little wooden pier. I began rowing against the wind. I pulled on the oars as hard as I could, but we made no progress. Soon the boat was riding up on shore.

"You're gonna have to row a little harder," Pa said as he again pushed us off from shore. Once more I tried rowing and just couldn't get anywhere. By now, the waves were splashing over the front of the boat.

"Look like our one-Apps-power boat doesn't have enough oomph to get us going," Pa said with a big grin on his face. "Guess we'll have to hang it up for the day. Always another day for fishing."

We loaded our gear back in the car, pulled the boat from the water, loaded it on the car, and drove away. The wind had won.

Wind also causes changes in barometric pressure that can affect fishing considerably. Sudden weather changes can bring about a feeding frenzy in fish, making it one of the best times for going fishing. Here are some generally agreed upon rules to follow regarding barometric pressure. When the pressure is rapidly rising, usually after a storm is past, fishing is poor. When a storm is on the way, barometric pressure usually drops, and fishing is good. Fish also get active and tend to be biting when the barometric pressure remains stable for several days.

Fishing ahead of a storm can provide good results, but doing so also creates challenging situations if you are out in a boat as bad weather, particularly lightning, approaches. The last place you want to be, no matter if the fish are biting, is in a boat on a lake in a lightning storm. At the first rumble of thunder, head for cover.

My brother Darrel recalls a time when he and Don got caught in a storm when they were boys. "One late spring day Don and I got our trout fishing gear and attached it to the bikes and began our trip to the Pine River," he remembers. "We hid our bikes in tall grass in the ditch along Milton Jones's road and walked down to the creek. We fished for a while and noticed that a big black cloud was coming out of the west. Shortly, we were hearing thunder and seeing lightning. We hurried to our bikes and began the two-mile trip home. As we rode up the hill by Bobby Mushinski's place, a bolt of lightning hit a tree right next to the road. The blast was so loud and the vibration so strong it nearly knocked us off our bikes as pieces of bark hit us and flew around us. By now it was pouring down rain and we were pedaling our bikes as fast as we could. We both knew that one of the most dangerous spots for lightning strikes was the high spot in the geography on Handrich's Hill, still a half mile away. We believed that lightning would not go through the rubber tires of our bikes, so we thought we should stay on the bikes and keep riding. The storm continued all the way home, with occasional bright light flashes followed by instant thunder. Once home, we were soaked and totally exhausted and ever so glad to be safe."

Temperature is also a factor in fishing. Most fish are cold-blooded and cannot regulate their temperature. Thus, they are forced to adjust to the water around them. Fish are more active in warmer waters and need more food to survive than when they are in colder water. In cold weather, fish become sluggish and move more slowly, thus needing less food to support themselves.[6]

Successful ice fishers, especially those who fish for northern pike with tip-ups and minnows, know about sluggish fish. Great patience is required. Ice fishers might get only two or three bites during an afternoon of fishing, as northern pike are slow moving in cold water.

~ FISH TALE ~

Windy Day on the Bay

My son-in-law, Paul Bodilly, comes from a long line of anglers. He shared this story.

My brother John has a big boat. I remember a day in June 2018, when he and I had planned a day of fishing for muskies on Green Bay. We hauled John's boat all the way from Madison to Green Bay. We picked up my sister and went to the boat landing. It was a windy day, and the waves were rolling in. I said, "We can't go out there, the waves are too high. Let's go to the other side of the bay. The wind's coming from that direction, and there should be fewer big waves." It took about a half hour to drive to the west side of the bay. When we got there, I said, "The bay's still too rough for fishing."

John said, "We drove all the way up here, and we're going fishing." We put the boat in the water. It was miserable on the bay. Trolling rigs just didn't work because of the high waves. The boat was going up and down and up and down. Waves smashed over the front of the boat. My sister said to me, "Tell John we must go back. He doesn't listen to me."

We finally convinced John that we had to get off the bay. It was a day to remember!

—Paul Bodilly

10

All About Bait

There is simply no fishing without bait. Bait is what attracts a fish to your hook. Most fish prefer live bait, such as minnows and worms. But many anglers use artificial bait, such as spoons, lures, and spinners, with great success. Choosing the right bait can be critical to catching fish.

Here is a general rundown of which fish prefer which kinds of live bait:

Earthworms: bluegills, trout, pumpkinseeds

Minnows: largemouth bass, walleye, trout

Leeches: largemouth bass, sunfish

Mealworms, waxworms: trout, sunfish, crappies

When I was a kid, the baits we most frequently used were nightcrawlers dug up from behind the chicken house and golden shiner minnows purchased from a bait shop in Wild Rose. As Darrel tells it, after ice fishing season ended one winter, we dumped a bucket of leftover golden shiners in the pond, hoping they would survive. They proliferated. Within a couple of years, the pond had become our main source of fish bait. All we had to do was catch them. Darrel remembers, "After ice formed on the pond, we chopped a rectangular hole in the ice and dropped a trap to the bottom, only three or four feet down. We baited the trap with oatmeal and saltine crackers inside open cheesecloth bags. Often, we would catch two to three dozen minnows each time we visited the pond."

Don remembers selling minnows for eighty-five cents a dozen to our fishing friends. He tells a story about a time when he was returning home after tending to his minnow traps, driving our 1941 Ford pickup on a slippery road. "I slid off the road and tipped the truck over in the ditch between Millers' farm and our place," he recalls. "A stump went right through the window on the driver's side. I crawled out of the truck and walked the rest of the way home. I had minnows in my hair and crushed crackers that I used for minnow bait stuck to my shirt. We drove the Farmall H tractor back to where the pickup lay on its side, hooked the chain on it and got it back on the road, and drove it home. The only thing broken was the window where the stump had gone through it. Didn't even dent a fender." (As is often the case with fish stories, Darrel has a different version of this memory. As he tells it, "There was lots of scratches and dents, but the truck was able to be driven home.")

The Nova Tackle shop became an important source for fishing lures. It was a special place, located on Main Street in Wild Rose, the back of the building crowding up to the millpond. The shop was all about fishing, from ice fishing to fly fishing. I remember one time when I went into the place as a kid and saw several women bent over work on little tables in the back. I asked Pa what they were doing. His answer: "They are tying flies."

I had no idea what that meant. Pa explained that the women bought squirrel tails for ten cents each and used them to make artificial flies for fly fishing. I immediately thought I must start saving squirrel tails when squirrel hunting season began in the fall.

Nova Tackle had just about everything an angler needed: casting rods, fly rods, all kinds of lures, and handmade flies. As a poor farm kid, I couldn't afford what Nova Tackle was selling and made do with the fishline, ten-cent bobbers, and hooks from Hotz's Hardware.

Whether you are an experienced angler or a novice, a bait and tackle shop is a place of wonder. They are often located near boat launches, piers, and lakes—but not always. A bait and tackle shop might be found in an auto repair shop, a gas station, or a convenience store. In addition to bait and tackle, they usually sell fishing licenses, along with six-packs of beer, soft drinks, and snacks. Of course, fishing advice is plentiful and free in most of these shops.

The walls of most bait and tackle shops hang heavy with colorful artificial lures of various shapes and sizes. In one corner of the shop, you'll usually find a small tank of water filled with minnows. Next to the tank, a refrigerator contains various kinds of worms boxed and ready for fishing. Many shops sell fishing rods and reels of various types and prices, along with nets and gaff hooks and other necessities for the serious angler. Ice anglers might find plain and fancy tip-ups and the latest in gasoline-powered ice drills.

Both seasoned and new anglers can improve their chances of fishing success by talking with the shop owners or staff about which kinds of bait or lure are working best for local fish at the moment.

NIGHTCRAWLER TALE

Have you ever been on a nightcrawler hunt? I wouldn't ask that of a trout fisherman, as nightcrawlers would not be his typical bait. (That said, I have learned there are two kinds of purists when it comes to flyfishing for trout: the authentic purist ties flies on his or her line; the practical purist fishes with flies until the fish

All About Bait

Sid Boyum captioned this drawing from opening day in 1967 "Memories of fishing seasons long gone by—hunting night crawlers with grandad."
FRIENDS OF SID BOYUM, COURTESY OF THE WISCONSIN HISTORICAL SOCIETY.
WHI IMAGE ID 123042

won't bite and then switches to nightcrawlers—but only if no one is watching.)

A nightcrawler is one of many types of earthworm. Nightcrawlers are the big ones, and they crawl around at night, especially after a warm spring rain. My son Steve became a great nightcrawler hunter.

One warm spring evening, after a brief rain shower, ten-year-old Steve and I armed ourselves with flashlights and set out on our first nightcrawler hunt of the season. Our first capture was a shiny, eight-inch-long specimen warming its underside on our concrete driveway. One scoop, and the worm was in my bait box. We proceeded along the garden hedge, letting the beam of light play where the bare soil met the grass.

"Hold it," Steve said as he made a grab for another. He stood up holding a crawler-shaped wooden stick.

Alongside the vegetable garden, I spotted a crawler in the outer ring of light. A quick grab, and I came up with a handful of mud. The next one I spotted caught the full beam of light and slid back beneath the surface before either of us could try for a capture. These creatures are extremely light-shy. Unskilled use of our flashlights caused us to lose at least a half dozen crawlers that evening. Our overall rate of capture was less than 50 percent.

We didn't know if our reaction time would improve with future hunts. Perhaps we could become purists and rely solely on flies for trout fishing. What we knew for sure: early-season trout love to nibble on big, fat nightcrawlers.

~ FISH TALE ~

A Bait Idea

My son-in-law Paul's sister, Jane Birr, lives in Green Bay and shared her early experiences ice fishing at the family's cabin on Lake Hilbert in Marinette County.

After watching my brother Billy ice fish for a few years, I thought I would try my hand at it all by myself. Wanting to be independent, I didn't ask him for any help as he sat in the toasty warm cottage eating a ham sandwich for lunch. I didn't dare ask him if I could use his gas-powered ice-drilling machine. I figured it would grab my clothes and twist me into the hole somehow. So off to the woodshed I went. The Wisconsin winter cold bit my cheeks, but I pressed on. I remembered from my youth that Dad had a super heavy, tall iron pole with a sharp wedge on the end that was used to whack holes in the ice. The woodshed door creaked open. It gave me the creeps in there. I envisioned mice and larger creatures lurking behind every piece of firewood. I jumped and hit my head on the low ceiling. What was that that just touched my leg? Relax, it was just the old toboggan I brushed against as I plodded to the back, grabbed the steel ice fishing chisel, and dragged it with all my might outside. I slammed the door before something could get me.

Man, this thing was heavy! And it was taller than me! I felt like Ahab going after the white whale or something. I had no idea how to set up a tip-up, so I thought I would find my little two-foot fishing pole that my dad gave me when I was little. I dropped the heavy iron ice chisel and rummaged around in the garage. There it was, up high on the fishing pole rack! I blew the dust off the little fishing pole and trudged into the deep snow, eager to complete my ice fishing mission.

On the way down to the lake, I made a quick stop in the cottage to grab a drink of water. Lugging that iron ice chisel around was making me thirsty! Billy looked blankly at me and said, "What are you doing?"

"I am going ice fishing," I said with confidence. All he said was, "That is ridiculous." He went back to his sandwich.

I dragged the ice chisel down all twenty steps and onto the ice. I picked a spot about two feet in front of the dock because the lake was making those scary contracting noises, and that was as far as I dared go. I dug away the snow with my hands and kicked with my moon boots to clear a spot on the ice. Then, with all my might, I lifted the heavy ice chisel and brought it down with all I had. A small piece of ice chipped away. That's it? Really? Up and down I hit. Over and over. One inch down . . . three inches . . . five inches. How thick was this ice, anyway? I was sweating profusely and thought that getting sucked into the ice by Billy's ice drilling machine might be a better option. But not willing to admit defeat to Billy, I pressed on. Eight inches ... ten inches ... my strikes were starting to get feeble. This was exhausting! Then I summoned all my strength, lifted the heavy ice chisel as high as I could, and WHACK! It went through the ice and almost took me with it, moon boots and all! Water bubbled up and filled the hole. Victory! I was elated! But my momentary joy was interrupted by a thought: What would I use for bait? It was the dead of winter so I couldn't dig for worms. I didn't have any minnows.

Back to the cottage I trudged. Now my sweat had started to freeze and I was cold. I went to the refrigerator and started digging around. There had to be something in there I could use. Lasagna? No. Bread? No. I didn't think it would stay on the hook. Definitely not salad. Then, there it was. A jar of pickled herring! Surely a fish must like pickled herring. I grabbed the jar and stood up victorious. I poured a few into a bag and then heard Billy ask, "What are you doing?"

"Well," I said, "I don't have any bait, so I thought I would use this pickled herring." He paused, looked at me in disbelief, and said, "That is absolutely ridiculous."

Not to be deterred, I grabbed the bag and off I went. It was hard getting that slippery little herring on to my hook. Besides that, my freezing cold fingers now smelled of pickled herring. I wiped my sweaty hair back, and now all I could smell was pickled herring. Finally, my hole was dug, the ice scooped out with my hand (which was by now completely numb), and there I stood jigging my pickled herring. Five minutes went by and nothing happened. Ten minutes. Nothing. I wished I had a chair. Jig, jig, jig ... nothing. I thought something would happen! For pride's sake I held on for thirty minutes before slowly walking back up the stairs to the cottage with my head down. With a big sigh, I went into the cottage only to hear Billy ask me, "Catch anything?" "No," I mumbled.

"Well, don't be ridiculous! Stay in here and warm up. I made you a dish of pickled herring!"

—Jane Birr

Years later, Jane Birr had much better luck ice fishing. Here she shows off a big northern she caught in 2021. BODILLY FAMILY PHOTO

11

Favorite Fishing Places

It was one of those mornings when the sun is pinkish red as it comes out from behind a massive cloudbank in the east. I'd returned to one of my favorite trout fishing places, the Wild Rose millpond, where I was intent on landing one of those big brown or rainbow trout that I knew were in there. The question was, would they bite? The weather was in my favor, warm for this time of the day, 5:15 a.m. There was barely a ripple on the pond's surface. I asked the age-old question, what should I use for bait? Should I try some flies, or maybe a popper? No fish seemed to be surfacing, so I discarded that idea. How about a shiny new French spinner? Or the rubber nightcrawler I'd gotten for Father's Day? The fake nightcrawler was attractive, but probably more attractive to wives looking for Father's Day presents than to a brown trout looking for breakfast.

Not being a purist in this game of trout fishing, I threaded a juicy, fat earthworm on my hook and let fling with my spinning rod. I gently eased the worm along the bottom of the pond, giving it a slight jerk, then another. Now it was six o'clock and my arm was getting a bit weary. I'd worn out three or four worms and had a kink in my elbow. Weren't the trout having breakfast today? Other anglers began to arrive. By six thirty, eight cars were parked by

Favorite Fishing Places

the old grist mill and fishermen were lining the bank of the pond. Nobody was catching fish, me included.

An early morning fishing trip is never a waste of time—that is, if you don't measure success by the number of fish caught. The robins were celebrating the beginning of a new day as if it were the first new day ever. That robin chorus alone was worth getting up early to hear. True anglers don't measure success by the number of fish they catch.

Sid Boyum drawing of an angler heading to his favorite fishing spot. FRIENDS OF SID BOYUM, COURTESY OF THE WISCONSIN HISTORICAL SOCIETY. WHI IMAGE ID 125059

Wisconsin offers a great variety of opportunities for anglers, from five thousand class I trout streams to fifteen thousand lakes of various sizes, plus our two Great Lakes. And over years of fishing, every angler finds his or her favorite place to fish. For some, it's a place that offers solitude and quiet time in nature. For others, it's the spot where they introduced their child to fishing and first saw a child's excitement after landing a fish. The beauty of a special fishing place often outshines the fish caught there.

Here are stories from some of my favorite fishing places.

LAKE GEORGE, RHINELANDER

For more than thirty years, I taught creative writing each summer at the School of the Arts in Rhinelander. Ruth and I rented a cottage on Lake George for the family to enjoy while I was teaching. In the evening, I was usually free to go fishing with the kids.

For three days during our 1972 stay at Lake George, there was no breeze. The temperature hung in the high eighties, and the humidity equaled it, strange weather for the Rhinelander area.

"Very unusual," the resort owner told us. "Often this lasts for a day or so; then it rains and cools off." But the sweltering heat continued, and the fish stopped biting, except for the occasional small perch or sunfish that might nibble on a worm.

Finally, great thunderheads grew in the west throughout the long, hot afternoon, then massed into a solid wall of violent weather. Lightning created jagged patterns across the darkening sky, and thunder echoed across Lake George.

We stood in our cottage, watching the rain blow across the lake. Our boat bounced at the pier, accepting the storm.

"Good time not to be on the lake," I said to my young fishing partners. They watched with me as several fishing boats scurried toward cover just as the first rush of wind and rain arrived.

As quickly as it started, the rain stopped. A stiff breeze blew from the northwest, and much cooler air sent wisps of steam from the lake.

"Let's try fishing," I said to the kids. I bailed water from the boat as they collected the fishing equipment.

"What do I use for bait?" Jeff asked.

"Try your bucktail spinner—northerns might be biting," I answered.

Jeff, who had just turned eight, had never caught a northern. Steve had caught his first northern ice fishing the previous winter. Slowly I rowed the boat toward some rushes, a likely place for a northern or perhaps even a muskie. Earlier in the week we'd heard about a youngster catching a 42-inch muskie on a bucktail lure.

"Drag the spinner out back of the boat as I row," I suggested.

As we neared the rushes, Jeff yelled, "Stop, my spinner is caught on something." I quit rowing. Then I saw the tip of Jeff's fishing rod jerk a couple of time. Steve saw it, too.

"You got a bite. You got a bite," Steve yelled. For a moment I thought the boys might jump out of the boat, they were so excited. After I got them calmed down, I tried to instruct Jeff on what to do. There were enough waves on the lake that the boat had begun drifting away from the rushes. I began rowing just enough to keep the boat in place. Jeff cranked on his reel. Two or three times I spotted the fish near the boat. Sure enough, it was a northern pike. Jeff tried to lift the northern into the boat with his rod, but the fish dropped back in the water. The next time Jeff brought the fish close to the boat, I slipped the net under it and brought it into the boat. Now the 20-inch northern was flopping in the bottom of the boat. To an eight-year-old accustomed to catching little perch and bluegills, it looked twice that long.

"Gee, he's a nice one, Dad," Jeff said. I agreed. Steve and I continued to fish while Jeff sat quietly admiring his first northern pike.

PESHTIGO RIVER

The Peshtigo River snakes through northern Marinette County, sometimes flattening out into a broad, slow-moving expanse, sometimes pounding rapidly over a rock-strewn bed on its way to Green Bay and eventually the Atlantic Ocean. It's a trout river—one of the finest in Wisconsin, or indeed in the nation. I fished on the Peshtigo nearly every year for a long time, matching my skills against the German browns, rainbows, and brook trout that have challenged me and other trout fishermen for generations.

For me, the trout always had the edge in the competition. There are undercuts in the Peshtigo's banks, deep holes behind rocks, and sunken logs—ideal hiding places for fish. The riverbank on either side is lined with aspen and birch. I spent far too much time retrieving my fishline from tree branches hanging low over the river. I always wore chest-high waders when I fished the Peshtigo, adding to the trout's advantage, for as I clumsily walked along the bottom of the river, trying to avoid hidden logs and slippery rocks, my mind couldn't concentrate fully on fishing. A misplaced foot, a misjudging of the current, and down I'd go. The waders would fill with water, and I'd spend the rest of the day drying out in front of the campfire.

But it was the setting that drew me back each year, not only the prospect of catching trout. I knew other places where I could catch more trout in less time. The lure for me was the gurgling and bubbling of the river, the trilliums in full bloom on the forest floor, the birds singing everywhere along the riverbanks. It was the opportunity to be alone in the outdoors, away from the press of people and technology. On the Peshtigo, I could put everything in my life back into perspective.

That's not to say that I didn't enjoy the pull of a German brown on my line. The thrill of fighting this river fish as it raced back and forth, trying to shake the hook caught in its lip, was hard to match.

The fish often won, and I'd feel the line go slack after a series of tugs and pulls. I would quickly cast again, trying to drop my baited hook in the place where the previous fight ended. Sometimes I succeeded in netting a beautiful specimen that would soon be sizzling in my cast-iron frying pan. But there might be one hundred casts before there was another bite.

Each trout is different, each cast, each bite, each fight. There are no hard and fast guidelines. This is one of the things I love about fishing. Each angler must discover for himself or herself how to catch a trout, and even then, we never know for sure that we're doing it the "right" way. The fast-moving Peshtigo, with its many twists and turns, has tried to teach me how to do it well.

NORWEGIAN LAKE

The old three-seater metal boat eased away from Anderson's landing on Norwegian Lake as I shoved an oar into the soft lake bottom and pushed hard. I fitted the oars in the oarlocks, and the boat gently moved forward, pointed toward the spot my two fishing companions, my dad and Steve, had mentioned as potential bluegill territory.

The lake was glassy smooth this early evening. The warm sun was still a long way from the horizon. Quietly, the old boat cut the water, the oars leaving little whirlpools that disappeared as the boat left them behind.

"This is about it," my dad announced. "Hold her still while I toss out the anchor." An old plastic one-gallon bottle filled with sand would serve as anchor. It was tied to one of the boat's seats with several lengths of baling twine.

"That anchor's not gonna hold," Steve said. But it did. We were fishing near the old marl hole. The makeshift anchor settled into the soft oozy material on the lake bottom, and the boat sat still. We had anchored on the edge of the deeply dredged hole so we could easily toss our lines into the depths of the dark green, almost black water.

Before I could tuck away the oars, my companions had their fishing equipment organized and were threading worms on their hooks. The first worm had hardly settled into the deep fishing hole when the bobber went skimming across the water's surface and then sank from sight. Steve's light spinning rod was bending toward the water, and soon a fat bluegill came flopping into the boat. Pa soon did the same—and all before I had tucked away the oars and grabbed up my fishing gear.

By the time I had joined the fun, three big bluegills were swimming in our catch pail. I tossed out my line—nothing. No action at all. My bobber lay motionless on the surface of the lake.

"You got your line in the wrong place," Pa said.

"You don't have to remind me," I answered.

I tossed my line where Pa pointed, and almost immediately I was catching bluegills, too. Some were too small to keep, but most were medium size—not bragging size, but still bound to be tasty after they were cleaned, rolled in flour, and fried in a cast-iron skillet with plenty of butter.

Then, no more bites. I yanked up the makeshift anchor and rowed the old boat about three hundred yards to the north shore. As the sun settled below the horizon, it painted the sprinkling of clouds a vivid lavender and threw the long shadows of the tamarack and pine trees lining the shore. I yanked the baling twine to loosen the anchor from the lake bottom and began rowing for shore. We had about twenty-five good-sized bluegills in the catch bucket.

"What a beautiful evening," I said as I rowed toward shore. My companions didn't comment, preferring to look and listen as nightfall slowly spread across the calm water.

~ FISH TALE ~

Surprise Catch

My brother Donald shared this memory of fishing on Norwegian Lake.

There were four of us in a boat that day. That's a boat full, as those boats were pretty small. We were fishing on the west side of the lake in a place called the ox hole, which was a deep spring hole where fresh water springs fed into the lake. Darrel's bobber went under, and he pulled up a great big snapping turtle! It about bent his cane pole in half. It was about the size of a big cast-iron frying pan. Upon seeing the big turtle, Pa said, "Cut the line, we don't want that turtle in the boat."

We all got a good look at the turtle while Darrel was pulling it toward the boat. It was dark gray, nearly black, and had a long tail. Its body was covered with bony plates. It had a long neck that was fully extended and the meanest looking head. After cutting the line, we watched as the big turtle slowly slid out of sight in the waters of Norwegian Lake.

—Donald Apps

Fish on Our Plates

Wisconsin's bountiful waterways have made fish a part of the state's diet since the first people lived on this land. Many anglers today practice "catch and release." This means that after the fish is caught (and after a picture is taken, if it's of "storytelling" size), they return it to the lake or stream. Others like to eat their catch. Fish are a nutritious, heart-healthy food, low in fat and rich in high-quality protein, omega-3 fatty acids, vitamin D, and riboflavin.

Those who eat fish should heed some cautions. According to Wisconsin Department of Natural Resources, the primary pollutants found in some Wisconsin waters are mercury and polychlorinated biphenyls (PCBs). These and other contaminants can accumulate in fish and, if consumed, can be harmful to our health. For more information and recommendations about how much and what types of fish are safe to eat, visit the page "Questions and Answers about Eating Fish" at dnr.wisconsin.gov.

THE FRIDAY NIGHT FISH FRY

"Where you going for fish on Friday?" It's a question asked by Wisconsinites no matter where they live in the state. The Friday night fish fry is a long-standing tradition here, and most people have their favorite—a nearby restaurant, supper club, church hall, or tavern that features fish along with all the trimmings. A typical fish fry menu consists of battered (often beer-battered), deep-fried bluegill, walleye, haddock, cod, or perch; French fries, potato pancakes, hash browns, or baby red potatoes; creamy coleslaw; plus a couple slices of rye bread, lemon wedges, and tartar sauce.

Food historians credit three things for creating Wisconsin's Friday night fish fry custom. First is the state's large Catholic population, many of whom avoid eating meat on Fridays. Second, during Prohibition, many supper club and tavern owners offered free or cheap plates of fish as a way to bring in business. And third, freshwater fish like perch, bluegills, and walleye were once plentiful and inexpensive here.[7] There are other theories for the fish fry's popularity as well, but whatever the reasons, the delicious custom is firmly embedded in Wisconsin food traditions, enjoyed every week throughout the state by thousands. Food and travel writer Mary Bergin has called the fish fry "regionally unique and a precious part of our state's culinary character."[8]

THE DOOR COUNTY FISH BOIL

If you've visited Wisconsin's Door County peninsula in the summertime, chances are you're familiar with the fish boil. While today it's known as a tourist attraction, the fish boil has humble, everyday beginnings, with roots in Lake Michigan's plentiful supply of whitefish and the need to feed large groups of workers cheaply.

The fish boil tradition was carried down through the years at family gatherings and churches. The Viking Grill in Ellison Bay is credited with starting the modern version of the fish boil in 1961. The White Gull Inn in Fish Creek began offering fish boils around the same time, and soon other Door County restaurants were offering fish boils as well. Referred to by one writer as "part culinary tradition, part performance, and part spectacle," a fish boil follows a traditional process. Locally caught whitefish are boiled in a large metal basket set inside a kettle. Step one: Add salt to the water in the kettle and bring it to a boil. Step two: Add potatoes. Step three: After the potatoes are cooked, add onions. Step four: Add pieces of Lake Michigan whitefish.[9]

Now comes the spectacular part. When the fish are nearly done, the boil master tosses kerosene on the fire, causing a burst

In this photo taken in Door County in 1967, hungry folks wait with anticipation for their delicious meal as the boil master finishes off the cooking process. WHI IMAGE ID 38351

of flames and a boil-over of the water in the cooking pot to remove the natural fish oils. The flames die down, and the meal is ready. The whitefish is served with melted butter, coleslaw, lemon wedges, and a large slice of Door County cherry pie.

FAVORITE RECIPES

With four generations of anglers in our family, we've cooked and eaten our share of fish. Here are some of our favorite recipes.

Basic Fried Fish

This recipe is a good one for preparing bluegills, perch, and other panfish for the table. Dip cleaned fish in milk. Sprinkle with salt, pepper, and paprika. Then roll in flour, cornmeal, cracker crumbs, or dried bread crumbs to coat. Heat oil or melted shortening in a pan. Add fish and cook over medium heat until fish is crisp and golden on the underside. Gently turn with a spatula and cook until the fish flakes easily with a fork. Total cooking time is about 8 minutes. Drain fish on paper towels and transfer to a platter. Keep warm until ready to serve.

Baked Fish

4 to 6 freshwater fish
Salt and pepper
¼ cup butter, melted
2 tablespoons lemon juice

Preheat oven to 350 degrees. Clean the fish and rinse well in cold water. Cut larger fish into fillets (smaller ones, like bluegills, can be left whole). Season with salt and pepper. Mix the melted butter and lemon juice. Put the fish in a greased pan and pour the butter and lemon juice mixture over the fish. Bake until the fish flakes easily with a fork, about 30 minutes.

Baked Fish with Bacon

4–5 slices bacon, uncooked
2 pounds fish fillets, cleaned
½ cup tomato soup or homemade tomato sauce
2 medium onions, sliced
Salt and pepper
Lemon slices

Preheat oven to 350 degrees. Place two slices of bacon in a greased baking dish. Place fish on top of the bacon. Cover with remaining bacon. Mix the tomato soup with enough water to make a sauce (or use tomato sauce). Add the sliced onions to the sauce, then add salt and pepper to taste. Pour carefully over the fish. Place lemon slices on the fish. Bake until the fish flakes easily with a fork, about 30 minutes. Check the dish during baking to be sure there is liquid in the bottom; add a little water if necessary. To serve, place fish on a platter with bacon and sauce from the pan.

Beer-Battered Fried Fish

1 cup flour
2 teaspoons garlic powder
½ teaspoon salt
⅛ teaspoon pepper
1 egg, beaten
1½ cups beer
2 cups crushed cornflake cereal or dried bread crumbs
1 pound fish fillets, cleaned and ready to fry
Oil for frying

Set up the fish-coating stations like this:
   Mix together the flour, garlic powder, salt, and pepper in one bowl.
   Mix together the beaten egg and beer in another bowl.
   Have the crushed cornflakes or bread crumbs ready on a plate.
   When everything is ready, prepare each fillet, keeping one hand "dry" for the flour bowl and crumbs plate and one hand "wet" for dipping into the egg and beer mixture. Place the fillet in the flour and lightly dust with flour mixture. Place fish in egg-and-beer bowl and turn to coat thoroughly. Dip the egg-coated fish into the crumbs and thoroughly coat all sides.
   Heat the oil in a large, deep skillet. Fry the fish, turning once, until both sides are golden brown and fish flakes easily with a fork. (Frying time depends on size of fillets.) Place fried fish on layers of paper towels while waiting to serve.

Pickled Fish

My dad was skilled at catching northern pike through the ice. He also enjoyed eating his catch, whether baked or pickled. Here is the recipe he followed for pickling fish.

Clean fish. Cut into pieces. Soak in salt water (1 cup of salt in 1 quart of water) for 24 hours.

Drain the fish and rinse. Soak in white vinegar for 24 hours. Save the vinegar for brine.

Combine 9 cups of vinegar (add more as needed), 2 cups of water, 1 cup of sugar, and 2 tablespoons of pickling spice and bring to a boil.

Pour brine over the fish and pieces of onions. "Ready to eat in 24 hours."

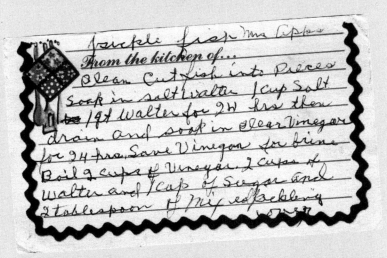

12

Boundary Waters Time

In far northern Minnesota, tucked up against the Canada border, is one of my favorite places to fish. The official name for the place is the Boundary Waters Canoe Area Wilderness (BWCAW). According to the USDA Forest Service, the BWCAW is over a million acres and extends nearly 150 miles along the international border. The area was set aside for recreation in 1926 and became part of the National Wilderness Preservation System in 1964. This is a land of moose and loons and wolves that howl in the night. It contains more than a thousand lakes, varying in surface area. And there are fish, especially smallmouth bass and northern pike.

Steve and I traveled to the Boundary Waters for the first time in 1983. I was forty-nine and on summer leave from my teaching position at the University of Wisconsin–Madison. Steve was twenty and a student at Winona State University in Minnesota. It was the beginning of a decades-long tradition for the two of us in which we left the city and all modern conveniences behind to sleep in a tent, paddle a canoe, warm ourselves by a smoky campfire—and do a lot of fishing.

The following memories are adapted from journal entries I made in the Boundary Waters over the years, starting with our first trip.

Tuesday, August 16, 1983

We are camping on a beautiful campsite on the east end of Binkshank Lake. We pitched our tent on a rocky little point that juts out into the lake. It's high enough so a breeze always seems to be blowing, and there are few mosquitoes or black flies, which is unusual, for they both are a menace during the summer in the Boundary Waters.

About seven this morning, four loons flew over our campsite, making their special wilderness call. We've seen a few ducks as we paddled our way to our campsite, as well as a huge bull moose. About 3 p.m. a light rain began falling. Fishing has been poor. A few bites, but nary a fish.

August 18, 1983, Thursday, 7 a.m.

I'm writing this while sitting on a rock outcropping that overlooks the lake. The sun is coming up over my left shoulder, but it will be a while before it peeks above the trees. There is a slight chop on the lake, caused by a southerly breeze.

As I sit here, I think about what makes this camping and fishing place different from the many other places where I have camped and fished. First, there are few people. Since Steve and I arrived here, we have seen no one. That means no loud parties, no yelling and loud laughing—all associated with a good party, but different from what we want while here.

There is no sound of background traffic. At night it is absolutely quiet, except for the lapping of the waves against the rocks below our campsite. Occasionally, a loon calls, breaking the silence. And then it is quiet again. What feelings do I have while here? A mixture of many. I am surprised that there still are places like this in the United States that are so beautiful and so unspoiled.

I'm also feeling a closeness to my oldest son, Steve. Ruth and I haven't seen him much since he has gone off to college and has been working at a youth camp in the summer. He's very quiet and seldom lets his feelings show. But it's clear he likes wilderness living as I do. Steve is well over six feet tall and strong. A good person to have on a wilderness canoe fishing trip as he does all the heavy lifting, including carrying the canoe across the portages.

August 19, 1983, Friday morning

About 2:30 a.m. a thunderstorm rolled into camp from the southwest. So much lightning that I was able to read my watch without my flashlight. The lightning flashes were so close together they appeared as one. The tent shook and shuddered but stood firm. Steve had pitched it well.

"Anything we should do?" I asked Steve as I sat up and checked to make sure the zipper on the tent door was properly closed.

"Go back to sleep, doesn't pay to worry about something you can't do anything about."

I felt around the tent door and grabbed my heavy shirt from the tent floor. It was soaked. The shirt had taken up the water which would have swept into the tent.

At 6 a.m. we awakened to a cloudy, windy day. After a light breakfast and a quick picking up of a wet tent and food containers, we were once more paddling. Our first portage, to Owl Lake, was only 50 rods. [There are 320 rods in a mile.] But the next one, to Tuscarora Lake, was 366 rods, which took us an hour and half of carrying the canoe and then walking back for our backpacks and doing it again.

On our camping-fishing trip in 1989, Steve and I were joined by Steve's friend Rick. It was Rick's first trip to the Boundary Waters.

July 27, 1989, Thursday evening

We are fishing on Fisher Lake. I gave Steve my new Rapala lure, and I gave Rick a spinner. I used a jointed Rapala. I soon caught a smallmouth bass. Steve caught a smallmouth bass, then a largemouth bass. Rick caught four smallmouth bass. By 4 p.m., when we left the lake, Steve had caught eight largemouth bass and six smallmouth bass. I had caught four. Several of the larger bass were a foot long and longer. We released all of them, but what a great afternoon of fishing it was.

A large snapping turtle lumbered through our campsite after supper. We watched it as it slowly made its way to the lake, first taking a drink of water. The turtle was maybe 15 inches in diameter and about a foot high. Its long tail had spikes like some prehistoric creature, and its back and legs were mostly black. Its front legs had long claws, and its neck, which it extended when it walked, was thick and snake-like. Its dark eyes watched every move we made. Its nostrils were two little holes between its eyes.

July 18, 1990, 6 a.m. John's Lake Campsite

The sun is just up over the trees to the east and the sky is clear except for a few whisps of clouds. A loon is a hundred yards or so away, floating on the glassy surface of the lake. She has two little half-grown loons floating behind her. I watched as one climbed on her back for a free ride. Then I saw a bald eagle dive bomb the loon and her little ones. The loon spread her wings and lifted her body from the water, dumping the little one on her back into the lake.

A battle took place between the eagle and the loon—the loon won. The eagle flew off and landed on a branch across the lake. The loon with her little ones continued to swim on the lake.

That afternoon, Steve and I paddled the length of John's Lake and portaged to Pike Lake, where we spent the afternoon fishing. We caught eight nice-size smallmouth bass. One weighed about 3 pounds or more, I would guess. It put up quite a fight before I landed it. It was fish for supper, with macaroni and cheese. A thunderstorm came up with thunder and lightning and even some hail. We ate the fish under the green kitchen tarp.

August 19, 1992, 7:30 a.m.

Last night the lake was so smooth and the night so dark that we could see star reflections on the water. It was like sitting between two skies.

A bit of surprise last evening when I was building the campfire after supper. A black bear came down the trail from the direction of the latrine. The bear and I looked at each other at a distance of about twenty feet. Then the bear, apparently not liking what he saw, wandered off into the woods in no hurry. I suspect the bear smelled our food and was in search of a free handout. Steve was fishing from shore and got to the see the bear as well. This was the first time in several years of wilderness camping that we had a bear visit our camp.

August 20, 1992

Steve and I finished supper. We had pudding and apple sauce for dessert and are now enjoying coffee. What a great camping trip—and what a terrible fishing trip. Today, Steve hooked a bluegill smaller than the lure he was using. Where are the smallmouth bass this year?

Many years later, as I reread these journal entries, I am reminded that fishing was an important reason for heading to the Boundary Waters each year. But there was so much more to those trips: being in a wilderness area immersed in nature, listening to the sounds of silence and the occasional call of loons, experiencing wonderful thunderstorms that thrilled, excited, and scared us. Upon returning to our jobs, we felt refreshed and renewed.

In the early years we traveled from lake to lake, making long portages. Starting in the early 1990s, we stayed at one campsite for the entire week. We discovered that we caught more fish if we camped on one lake and then spent our time fishing in that lake and nearby lakes. Besides, as we both were getting older, lots of paddling and portaging was not as much fun as it had been when we were younger.

For many years we traveled to the Boundary Waters the week after Labor Day, happily avoiding the big crowds of summer. We continued to make our Boundary Waters trip every year until 2012. I was seventy-four that year, and Steve was forty-nine. He had injured his back and was unable to portage the canoe.

Here are journal entries from the later years at the Boundary Waters, when we did more fishing. Nearly all of it was catch and release.

Fishing in the Boundary Waters, 2007. PHOTO BY STEVE APPS

August 25, 1994

Reflections on the Boundary Waters. I saw several satellites moving across the sky and concluded that it is nearly impossible to leave behind the influence of mankind. But this place comes close. Here there are no condos, no summer homes, just hundreds of acres of trees, lakes, and wilderness. This is the home of the black bear and the loon, the bald eagle, and the ever-present red squirrel. As I write this, I hear a loon calling, the sound echoing across the lake. The lake is smooth and sound carries for a great distance. A cloud bank is building in the west—rain again today.

August 28, 1997

Today Steve suggested we fish farther away from camp. We stopped to fish at the portage where yesterday I had caught a 14-inch smallmouth bass. My first cast: another 14-inch smallmouth. We each caught two smaller ones before portaging to Canoe Lake and then to Crystal Lake. No more fish until we returned to where we'd caught the nice ones near the first portage. We caught a couple more little ones before we returned to camp.

August 25, 1998

After picking up our nonresident fishing licenses in Grand Marais and our camping permit at the ranger station, we drove to our designated entry point and began paddling to our assigned camp site on Pine Lake. By the time we got to Pine Lake the wind had come up and it was a long, hard paddle to our camp site. The lake was too rough for fishing, so we sat by our campfire, reading and listening to the water pound the rocks. Enjoying the outdoors. So peaceful. Steve took a short swim, but the water was very cold. I stayed on shore.

August 19, 1999

Foggy this morning, can't see across the lake. Lots of dew on everything. Fishing has been excellent this year. We've already caught sixteen smallmouth bass ranging from 7 to 16 inches. Steve caught the largest one of all last night, more than 16 inches. We think we have hit a record for the most fish caught in all of the years that we've been coming here. We both practice catch and release after recording the information.

Saw a family of otters this morning, five of them swimming by our campsite. What wonderful swimmers they are, and they seem to have so much fun as a family. Saw a beaver last night, too, swimming by. And not to forget the loons and seagulls we see regularly.

September 5, 2000

We are camping on Pine Lake, about a mile from the portage. The campsite is on a rocky hill. It is a clear, cool day with lots of sunshine and a little breeze. Steve pitched his new North Face tent near the water. I pitched my little L.L. Bean dome tent farther up the hill. We've seen no other canoeists since we arrived. Completely quiet except for the loons calling.

September 6, 2000

This morning I was greeted by a double rainbow when I crawled out of my tent. I remember the old saying: Rainbow in the morning, sailors take warning. And then it started, a cold rain. No mosquitoes, just the sound of rain on the tent roof. Waiting for it to stop so we can go fishing.

August 9, 2001

The first crack of thunder woke me up a little after 2 a.m. Then for an hour the wind blew and the sky crackled with lightning. The thunder roared and the rain fell. The tent shuddered at times, but it stayed in place. This is as close as being outside in a thunderstorm, without actually being out in it. The experience is exhilarating and frightening, awesome and awful. When it was over, I was happy to have been there. But when I was in the midst of it, I didn't know if a tornado was coming, a hailstorm, or a strong-wind tree smasher.

After breakfast, I saw a break in the clouds to the west. The rain stopped, and we once more climbed in the canoe for a day of fishing, after a night of little sleep. This is our last day in the Boundary Waters for this year. I reflect a bit on what the Boundary Waters has to offer:

solitude,
loon magic,
wicked thunderstorms,
generally good fishing,
outstanding scenery,
and a week with my son.

September 3, 2008, Wednesday

In the forties this morning with a stiff northwest wind that makes it seem even colder. I am wearing long underwear, pants, thin shirt, heavy shirt, hooded sweatshirt, and rain jacket over everything. I am sitting under the dining shelter, mostly comfortable. We are hoping the wind goes down so we can take the canoe out fishing later this afternoon.

Steve caught a 12- to 13-inch northern from the campsite. Skinny thing it was.

September 4, 2008, Thursday

Temp in the thirties. During the night I woke up shivering. I'd let the sleeping bag slip down from my shoulders. Got up and put on more clothes. Slept well after that. Awakened to a foggy day on the lake. Dead quiet. No wind. Red squirrel chattering away as I prepared breakfast.

Finally got to go fishing in midafternoon. We canoed down a stream to a small, secluded lake. Canoed though a big patch of wild rice that was not quite ripe. Steve caught two northern pike, one about 13 inches long and the other about 18 inches. I caught a foot-long perch and a 15-inch northern. Northern pike are always fun to catch. Even the little ones are great fighters.

Steve had a new lure for this fishing trip. It had an orange top and a gold middle. So far on this trip, using this new lure Steve caught four northerns, three smallmouth bass, and one perch. Twice a big fish broke his line, but each time we were able to retrieve his lure as it floated.

13

More Adventures on Ice

The ice chips jumped from the hole as I pounded the ancient ice chisel into the lake ice. The chisel was same old one used by my dad, made some fifty years ago from a Model T Ford axle and sharpened on one end by the local blacksmith. Finally, the chisel punched through the six inches of ice on Mt. Morris Lake. The chisel was heavy, so I only needed to lift it and let it fall to chop an ice fishing hole. One needs some experience to direct the blows in such a way to make a hole large enough to let through a 20-pound northern pike, yet small enough so the crossbars on the tip-up have room to rest on the edge of the hole.

The ice chips fell on already slippery ice, making the task of standing a challenge. I had a leather thong wrapped around my wrist, insurance against dropping the old chisel in the lake. Two or three other times the chisel had fallen in, and the remainder of an otherwise good fishing day was spent retrieving the implement using long pieces of wire.

With a rush and a gurgle, water filled the hole as the chisel punched through the last inch of ice. A few more well directed chops, a couple of swipes with the ice strainer, and I was ready to place a tip-up over the hole, its line going deep into the water.

The sun was bright this particular morning, the temperature in the twenties. The ice glistened as my dad and brothers and I stood

My father on the ice in the 1980s.

with our backs to the wind, which was coming briskly across the lake as we watched for tip-up action. The ice was talking, snapping, cracking, groaning, and forming pressure cracks. I remembered how frightened I had been when I was a kid and saw the ice crack beneath my feet. I thought that surely I would fall into forty feet of water and be lost forever.

We had walked more than a half mile on slippery ice to this fishing spot. So, we were quite content, after setting up the tip-ups, to relax and stand around and wait for some fishing action. We had gotten to the lake by ten in the morning, and there were but three or four other fishermen on the lake. By eleven, twenty more had arrived. Periodically, someone would yell "tip-up" and run, slip, and slide toward the fish hole where the tip-up flag was up and flying in the breeze. I could spot the more experienced ice fishers by how they ran on slippery ice. They used a kind of skating motion.

That morning everyone seemed to be catching fish, but at noon the weather began to change. What had started out as a beautiful sunny day was fast becoming cloudy and the temperature was dropping. By one thirty, a few flakes of snow began filtering down, and an hour later it was snowing so hard it was nearly impossible to see the tip-up flags.

The fish seemed to sense the weather change as well. Few tip-up flags were flying up. But even with the snow, it was a picture-book day. When the snowflakes began falling, the wind quit blowing, allowing for the extreme quiet that often accompanies a snowfall. I could hear fishermen halfway across the lake, their voices magnified by the weather conditions.

Fearful of the driving conditions, we began the long, slippery, half-mile hike back to the car with three northern pike, our take for the day. Some of the fishermen had been more successful than we, some less so. All of us would be back another day. Ice fishing does that to its followers.

ICE FISHING CAMPFIRE

Sitting by a campfire is always a pleasant experience, especially so when the temperature drops below zero and there are several inches of snow on the ground. Keeping warm is a challenge when you are ice fishing on such a day; a person just can't wear enough clothing to keep warm.

The old-timers I knew who enjoyed sitting by smoky campfires on the shores of ice-covered lakes would often say, "A campfire warms a person twice: once when he cuts the wood, and again when he burns it." I would add that the ice fisher is warmed a third time, as he or she searches for downed trees, dry leaves, and dead grass to start the campfire.

On one trip to Mt. Morris Lake, we learned after the first chilling half hour that we needed a campfire or we'd spend the day waving our arms and stamping our feet to keep warm. We were only a short distance from a place on shore where trees came down to the water's edge. After a bit of exploring, we found a spot where someone had built a fire the previous day. The site was on a small rise, allowing us a good view of our tip-ups. I gathered an armful of dead marsh grass that stuck through the shore ice and pulled some dry oak leaves from a nearby branch. To this collection, I added a few finger-size oak twigs. I piled the twigs into a little teepee over the grass and leaves and touched a match to the upwind side. After a brief moment of indecision, the flame burst into action. I tossed a few larger sticks on the fire as we got comfortable sitting on an old fallen tree that our predecessor had wisely used as a backdrop for the fire site. There is something about watching tip-ups through the smoke of a small campfire that makes the ice fishing experience complete. Occasionally the wind shifted, and I get a solid whiff of oak smoke, enough to make my eyes water as I waited for the wind to change direction again.

Even sandwiches taste better when eaten around a campfire. Maybe it's because the fire's warmth allows me to hold the sandwich with my bare hands. A sandwich loses some of its flavor when held by a heavy mitten that smells of minnows and northern pike.

A light snow began to fall in the early afternoon. Each flake disintegrated with a sizzle as it struck the campfire. Eventually I quit searching for firewood and allowed the campfire to turn into coals. When all that remained of the fire was a few flaky gray ashes, we knew it was time to leave. We warmed our hands one last time over the remnants of the fire and walked out on the lake to gather up our fishing gear.

RIVER ICE FISHING

"Want to try some ice fishing on the Mississippi?" my brother-in-law Burton Olson asked me on a chilly day in February 1968.

"Ice fish on the mighty Mississippi?" I answered with considerable skepticism. "What do you catch?" For me, the Mississippi had always been a watery road for towboats pushing coal and grain barges. "Is the ice safe?" I added.

My brother-in-law assured me that in the backwater where we would fish, the ice would be quite safe. After a little more encouragement—it doesn't take much—we were off to La Crosse and the Mississippi to catch fish through the ice.

About two dozen other ice fishers had gathered in the backwater spot where we were fishing. They were chatting about past fishing excursions and the beautiful winter day.

Along with an ice chisel, we had brought typical panfish gear—short poles with monofilament line, a small bobber, and couple of split shot squeezed on the line just above the hook. We would use inch-long minnows for bait.

I worked up the courage to ask again, "What kind of fish might I expect to catch?"

"Oh, mostly crappies, but last week a fellow hooked a northern pike that ended up smashing his fishing rig," my brother-in-law answered.

"What's the river bottom like here?" I asked.

"We're fishing in what was once a gravel pit that's now filled with water. There are dead trees here, as well."

He was right. I snagged my hook on something the first time I tried to check on my minnow. After a couple of jerks, I pulled up a small twig. Crappies were drawn to the security of the buried tree branches. After a bit of bobber adjusting to hit the proper depth, just off the bottom, we began catching crappies. They were large ones, most larger than a man's hand. About every ten minutes we caught one. Soon we had fifteen of the silver beauties.

What I learned that day: You can catch crappies in the oddest places, even through the ice in a gravel pit filled with Mississippi River water.

~ FISH TALE ~

First Time Ice Fishing

Son-in-law Paul's sister, Jane Birr, shares her early experiences ice fishing at the family's cabin on Lake Hilbert in Marinette.

I never had gone ice fishing before, but I started getting reeled into it watching my older brother Billy at the cottage. He would open the door, letting the freezing cold winter air in, and yell "Tip-up! Tip-up!" Billy's wife, Susie, would stuff five-year-old Shannon and her little sister Emily into their snowmobile suits as I quickly pulled on my old and faithful moon boots and warm red jacket. Into the dark we raced to follow Billy down the twenty icy steps to the lake as his headlamp lit the way. Stars like fireflies lit up the night sky as we stepped onto the ice. Our hearts raced, first from the ice contracting, sounding like the call of humpback whales, and second from our hopes of what awaited us at the tip-up.

We arrived at the eight-inch hole and all fell to our knees surrounding it. What lurked below in the deep, pulling out the string of black line? Then Billy surprised us with, "Shannon, I want you to pull this one in." "Really, Daddy, really?" Oh, my. Off came her little gloves, and Billy instructed her to pull in the black line hand over hand. The fish had taken out a lot of line, and we wondered if it was still there. Then Shannon exclaimed, "Daddy, I feel something pulling!" Her little head was getting pulled closer and closer to the hole as the battle lingered on. "Pull, Shannon! Pull!" we screamed as Emily looked on with very wide eyes. This was all so exciting! So mysterious. So different from normal fishing. Then, Billy exclaimed, "I see it, Shannon! It's huge." One more big pull! She yanked back with everything she had, and lo and behold, a 25-inch behemoth northern pike popped onto the ice out of that little hole. I had never seen anything like it! We were all so excited and cheered in delight as Billy had Shannon hoist up her prize for a picture and a memory for the ages.

—Jane Birr

14

Fishing with Friends

Some anglers like to fish alone, preferring to enjoy the out-of-doors, the quiet, the subtle sounds, smells, and sights of nature without other people around. Others, myself included, enjoy fishing with family and friends, sharing the experience and telling stories of other fishing adventures. Here are stories of some of my favorite times spent shared with fishing companions.

My brother Don accompanied me on this opening day of trout season in 2005.

CANADIAN ADVENTURE WITH HELGI

It was hot that mid-August day in 1967, close to eighty-five degrees, with no breeze to ripple the lake's surface. And it was only 10 a.m. What would it be like by afternoon? Our family vacation had taken us to Winnipeg, Manitoba, to visit friends from my college days. Helgi Austman and I wanted to fish for northern pike and had picked Lake St. George, about 175 miles north of Winnipeg. Helgi assured me, with a bit of a smile, that nobody's ever been skunked on Lake St. George.

Lake St. George is about twelve miles long and a couple miles wide. Black spruce and white birch come down to the water's edge. Several large islands, also heavily wooded, break up the monotony of the lake. No cottages lined the shores then. Only two people lived on the lake this time of year, Helgi told me, the forest ranger who ran the fire tower and Lee Chapman, who operated the White Birch Resort. In winter, no one lived there.

We stopped at the resort and rented one of Chapman's homemade boats, powered by an Oshkosh-made 10-horsepower Mercury motor. Chapman had been a successful Winnipeg businessman who grew tired of the rat race (his words) and moved to Lake St. George. He was thirty-five miles from a mailbox, a telephone, electricity, a grocery store, and a neighbor.

He greeted us with, "You've come the wrong time of year for Jack." That's what Chapman called northern pike. "It's just too hot. They're all hiding in the weeds, not feeding."

I handed him $6.50 in Canadian money for a nonresident fishing license and bought a few chocolate bars, and then Helgi and I climbed into the boat for a try. Maybe Chapman was wrong about the Jack not biting.

Loons sounded off across the bay from us, an eerie laugh that still stands my hair on end when I hear it in the middle of the night. A couple hundred yards to the right, two large pelicans were enjoying the summer day. They looked at us cautiously and then decided to fly off in front of us. I got a good look at their large lower beaks, white bodies, and black-tipped wings. I hadn't realized pelicans were so beautiful.

I tied a small red-and-white spoon on my six-pound test spinning line and threw it over the side. It was legal to motor troll for northerns, so we slowly worked our way along the lake shore, our lures trailing behind the boat.

Lake St. George is a nesting place for mallard and canvasback ducks, and they were out on their morning search for food. No doubt they were already getting prepared for their trip south, through Wisconsin, on their way to their winter home away from cold and snow.

"Stop the boat, I'm snagged," I blurted out. The snag started to jerk, and the drag on my reel engaged. I reeled in a 16-inch northern! Helgi said the fish should grow some more, so I released it back in the lake. Every fifteen minutes or so, one of us had a bite. Sometimes the bite was a miss, but by four thirty we had boated fifteen fair-size northerns—the largest was 28 inches and weighed probably 5 pounds. Helgi thought the fishing was terrible. "We should have had forty fish by this time," he grumbled. I was pleased. I hadn't had such a good fishing day in a long while.

We pulled the boat up on shore and immediately set about cleaning the fish we had caught. The Manitoba Conservation Department provided a fish cleaning board setup, complete with a pail to catch the cleanings. With our fish cleaned and filleted, we started a campfire and heated a cast-iron skillet. We soon were eating the tastiest fried northern fillets I had ever eaten.

When we started back for the cabin after 9 p.m., the sun was still high in the western sky. Helgi told me that in mid-June in those parts, the sun doesn't set until after 11 p.m. The loons were at it again as we headed south to Chapman's resort to return the boat. We told him about our catch for the day. His parting words: "Why don't you come back when the fish are biting? Sounds like you had a bad day."

WOLF RIVER ADVENTURE WITH MYRON

I got to know Myron Johnsrud when he came to Wisconsin from North Dakota to attend graduate school at the University of Wisconsin. Myron had fished the Garrison Dam reservoir in North Dakota, but he had never fished for trout. He wanted to give trout fishing a try, so I took him along on a trip to the Wolf River in Menominee County.

When we left Madison, the weather report was a bit dicey: scattered showers and cool. We selected a campsite at Wolf Rapids in the northern part of the county. The river ran just behind our tent, like in pictures I had seen in fishing magazines. The campsite was primitive; the one facility was an outhouse. Firewood was available in the form of dead pine branches, and any water we needed would come from the river.

We arrived late on a Friday afternoon and immediately tried some fishing before setting up camp. We should have saved our energy. Neither of us had a bite. Soon my brother Donald arrived with a friend. We set up my old umbrella tent and searched for a place where we could cook our meals. The fresh air, aromatic with pine, had sharpened our appetites to an edge.

Out came the camp stove and the cooking kit. In a few minutes, we had a pot of pork and beans and a kettle of potatoes boiling. "How many brats should I fry?" my brother asked. Soon twenty large brats were shrinking and turning a golden brown over the dull gray fire. For coffee, I brought river water to a boil and carefully dumped coffee grounds into the water and let it bubble until someone said, "That looks about right." We let the grounds in the brew settle. It took me back to the farm and my mother's boiled coffee. Beans, boiled potatoes, brats, and a couple cups of coffee tasted like a banquet meal.

After eating, we pulled on waders, strapped on our creels and landing nets, and headed for the river. Myron had never worn waders, and he didn't have a net, so we decided to stay close to each other in case he caught a keeper that required the net. Wading didn't bother Myron. Some people get dizzy standing in hip-pocket-deep water with a strong current tugging at their knees, trying to wash them downstream. But not Myron. He adjusted like a pro—perhaps because he had been a US Air Force jet pilot. Somehow, he saw a relationship between sloshing along the river bottom fighting the current and nosing a jet fighter plane through a thunderstorm. He told me one of the things he liked most about flying was the challenge of chasing up the steep side of a thunderstorm as if it were a mountain. Keeping your balance while standing in the Wolf River was a similar kind of challenge.

On my third cast, I hooked a fish that broke water but otherwise didn't act like a trout. I landed a 15-inch northern pike, using a number-ten hook, four-pound test line, and an earthworm for bait!

The Wolf River is full of surprises. Later, I caught two smallmouth bass but still no trout. Myron had a few strikes but caught no fish. By now it was dark. We stoked the campfire. It snapped and crackled as pine will do. We sat around the little blaze, sharing our experiences and enjoying another cup of boiled Wolf River coffee.

HELEN LAKE PADDLE WITH MAURY

My neighbor Maury White and his wife, Grace, invited Ruth and me to spend a weekend with them at their Vilas County cabin. The first evening, Maury suggested we go fishing in 102-acre Helen

Lake, not far from the cabin. To get to Helen Lake, Maury and I canoed about a half mile down Helen Creek, winding through swamp and marshland and around islands of cattails and floating pond lilies. After fifteen minutes or so of paddling, we turned a corner, and we were on Helen Lake.

The lake was surrounded by church spire spruce, white birch, and red and white pine. No cottages, resorts, or piers broke the isolation. We heard no sounds other than the gurgling of water as the canoe paddles dug into the lake's smooth surface.

"Better get your fishing gear ready," Maury suggested. I tucked my canoe paddle under the seat and tied an artificial minnow on my six-pound-test spinning line. Maury was not a fisherman, but he enjoyed the out-of-doors. He agreed to paddle while I trailed my bait behind the canoe. As we moved past a little peninsula, we glimpsed two deer hurrying up the hill from the lake. A family of ducks swam a few hundred yards from us.

I felt a nibble on my line. "Must be a weed," I said. But then it jerked again, and I reeled in an 8-inch perch. "I thought there were no fish in this lake," I kidded my canoe-paddling friend. "Still, this is the kind of fish you expect to catch with a cane pole and a worm."

I tossed the lure back in the water. Just a few feet farther and the line was tugging again. This time I could tell something bigger than a perch was going after my bait. I yelled, "Quit paddling" and began cranking on my reel as the drag let out monofilament line faster than I could reel it in. The battle was brief. A fair-sized walleye gave up and allowed me to bring it into the canoe.

"This is more like it," I said to my smiling companion. A few yards more, and I brought another walleye into the canoe. The sun cast long shadows of the spruce on the glass-smooth water. A red squirrel chattered from its perch on a low-hanging birch branch as we paddled past.

We came to a rocky shoreline where the water seemed to drop out of sight. I felt another solid grab at my artificial minnow.

And then another. I missed both of them but then caught a third walleye.

"Let's paddle past that place again," I suggested. We did, and I caught one more.

"Do you suppose I might catch my limit of walleyes?" I asked. "Only one more to go." Maury dug in his paddle, and we silently moved to another rocky shore that looked like a possibility for more fish. It was. As soon as we entered the cove, I caught a fifth walleye. In two hours and one turn around Helen Lake, I had my limit of walleyes. What more could a fisherman ask for?

"Look over there," Maury said, pointing a paddle toward the opposite shore. Two deer were leisurely drinking water, completely ignoring the silver canoe and its two occupants. We paddled the canoe back toward Helen Creek, quite satisfied with the two hours we had spent in this quiet place in Vilas County. I would like to try Helen Lake again, in early spring or October, when the walleyes are supposed to be "really biting."

FISHING IN THE RAIN WITH PA

The day was a mix of sunshine and thunderclouds in late June. I took my dad, then ninety-one, fishing on Gilbert Lake. I had trouble getting my old 4-horsepower Johnson motor started, but it eventually revved to life, and we chugged across the lake. The little motor wasn't very powerful, but it beat rowing. We arrived at our fishing spot, and I tossed the anchor over the side. Almost immediately I heard a clap of thunder, and it began raining—raining hard. I put on my rain gear and hunkered down. Pa put a five-gallon empty pail over his head and lay the boat cushion on his lap. The thunderstorm was brief, but it rained enough that my feet got wet in the bottom of the boat. We didn't catch any fish. Still, we had a great time fishing, and I've never forgotten the image of my dad sitting in the boat with a pail on his head.

~ FISH TALE ~

Fishing with Uncle Jim

My son-in-law Paul Bodilly's brother-in-law, Larry Wellenstein, tells this story about fishing as a young man with his Uncle Jim—proof that fishing with others isn't always the most pleasant experience.

My Uncle Jim had planned a week fishing in the northwestern part of the state, and his usual partner canceled. Dad wanted me to go with Jim, so I did. Not having spent more than a couple hours at a time with this bachelor uncle at family gatherings, I had no idea what to expect.

We spent a quiet five-hour ride towing Jim's aluminum boat behind his 1960 Plymouth. We arrived late and had a bite to eat at a bar where we rented a cabin for our four-night stay. I soon learned that my uncle took fishing very seriously.

Each day we got up at 5 a.m. and were on a lake before 6. Absolutely no talking was allowed, lest we scare the fish. Jim bought sweet rolls to snack on for our breakfast, and one bottled drink was allowed per outing. Each day we fished until 10 or 11 and then came in to find a place to eat lunch and buy groceries for the next morning's breakfast. At about 2 p.m., we went out on the lake again and fished until dark.

The first day, I caught nothing, and Jim caught a couple of small northerns. I learned his foolproof way of baiting a hook and how to secure worms and minnows and leeches so they won't fly off with the first cast. We ate at a different bar each night and then went to bed. We fished a different lake each day. For two of the four days we fished the entire day in the rain. On those days we came in before dark to dry our clothes on the kerosene heater so they would be ready the next morning. I don't recall bringing any fish back home.

In the future I willingly went on half-day trips with Uncle Jim, usually on Sunday afternoons after Jim sang in the choir at St. Mary's of Lake Church. One afternoon when I was a junior in high school, he had me get in the boat as he unhooked it from the trailer at a Sheboygan River landing. He didn't count on the boat sliding out as far as it did into the current, and I spent the most frantic ten minutes of my life finding the oars and rowing with all my might to overcome the current carrying me toward a waterfall. I beached it less than one hundred feet from disaster.

Jim never apologized for what I went through that day or complimented me on what I did to save myself and his boat, motor, and gear from going over the dam and down the Sheboygan River. I caught one nice crappie and an attitude toward him that day. The next few summers I declined most fishing opportunities unless they were after-supper trips to a small local lake. I can't say I enjoyed any of the sitting still and quiet for hours at a time, but I usually brought back at least one bass, and my dad was happy that his brother had my company and I got to go fishing when my dad couldn't take me.

—Larry Wellenstein

Learning to Fly (Fish)

My son-in-law Paul's friend Bret Schultz is a longtime ardent fly fisherman. He shared some valuable tips—and reassurances—for those looking to try this specialized form of fishing.

When I first ventured into the fly fishing world, it was intimidating. Forty years ago, there was next to no one who fly fished in the

This Sid Boyum drawing from 1964 depicts a fly fisherman hooking a lunker bass. FRIENDS OF SID BOYUM, COURTESY OF THE WISCONSIN HISTORICAL SOCIETY. WHI IMAGE ID 123040

small village where I grew up. One had to learn through reading books and magazines and lots of trial and error. For beginners today, learning has never been easier. With the internet, social media, fly shops, and various outdoor clubs, you can reduce your learning curve by years.

The first step: getting the right tackle and supplies. Yes, it can be a scary adventure, but it doesn't have to be. Most if not all major tackle dealers now offer starter outfits consisting of a reel, rod, line, and leader. Rods in various lengths and line weight classes are available. If I had to pick just one, I would choose an eight- or eight-and-a-half-foot rod that throws a five-weight line, a size that should be able to handle trout, panfish, and bass. Other essentials include tippet material in 3, 4, and 5x, nippers, fly floatant, and forceps. You may also want waders; options are knee-high, hip, or chest.

Next, you will need some flies. At first, choosing which fly to use where and when can be a challenge. There will likely be a fly shop near where you are going to fish. Stop in or call and tell them where you plan to fish and your targeted species, and they will recommend the appropriate flies. Thankfully, there are some old standbys, both surface and subsurface, that will usually catch fish most anywhere.

After some experience, you will find flies that work for you in your typical situations. Confidence in the fly you tie on means more than you might think. As anglers, we tend to fish better when we believe in the pattern that we tie on. I typically fish a dozen streams within an hour of home. I have learned from experience that there are about a dozen fly patterns, both surface and subsurface, that will take fish throughout the season. Time spent on the water will be your best teacher. Look at shoreline vegetation, poke under in-stream rocks, and investigate bugs that are present on or above the surface for clues to what the fish are feeding on.

There is one factor that is even more important: practice. Long before your first trip, take the time—lots of time—to practice your casting. I cannot overstate how important practice is for your ability to put the fly in the right location in the moment. I could take you

DUNKING IN GILBERT LAKE

According to the Wisconsin Department of Natural Resources, Gilbert Lake is 139 acres, with a maximum depth of 65 feet. This lake, located between Wild Rose and Waupaca, was one of my dad's favorite fishing spots, and we fished it often. There we caught a variety of fish: largemouth bass, smallmouth bass, walleye, northern pike, perch, bluegills, and sunfish.

If I wasn't fishing for trout on opening day of fishing season, I often headed to Gilbert Lake. One memorable opening day, the temperature was chilly, maybe in the fifties, and a cool breeze blew from the northwest. I was in my early eighties, and it had become a bit difficult for me to climb into a regular boat with relatively high sides, like my 12-foot aluminum boat. Donald and I decided to take out his 14-foot flat boat. The boat had flat sides and pedestal seats that made for comfortable riding and fishing. The boat also had a 15-horsepower motor and a small electric trolling motor, so no rowing was required.

We put the boat in at the public landing on the east end of the lake. There were only a handful of boats on the lake, so we had our choice of where we would go. We headed toward a favorite spot on the northwest corner of the lake, maybe a hundred feet or so from shore, where we had caught largemouth bass in the past. As we motored there, I zipped up my winter jacket to keep out the cold. Don killed the motor, and the boat floated toward what he considered the exact place we wanted to be.

Chilly temperatures aside, it was a reasonably nice opening day. I heard birds chattering in the trees that surround the lake. "Wonder what's biting today?" Donald asked. I put my hand in the water to check the temperature. "Water's a bit cold," I said. The breeze blowing from the northwest rocked the boat slightly.

"Yup, it is," Donald said. "Ice has been out only a few weeks. Expect the water is probably in the low fifties, maybe colder."

We drifted a few more feet, and Donald asked, "Can you toss in the anchor? This seems like the right place."

I put down my fishing rod, got up from my pedestal seat—and lost my balance as I tried turning toward the anchor resting on the bottom of the boat. I grabbed for the seat, and it broke off. I fell into the lake with a huge splash. Even though I was wearing a life vest, I must have gone almost to the bottom of the lake, maybe twenty feet deep. I immediately popped back to the surface, spitting lake water. Bobbing on the surface, with my life vest keeping me afloat, I saw the most surprised look I had ever seen on Donald's face. I heard him say, "What'd you do that for?"

"Get me out, I'm freezing," I said. I gave him my hand and he began pulling, but he just couldn't get me into the boat. My soaked clothing made me too heavy. Donald started the trolling motor, but it wasn't strong enough to move the boat with my weight hanging on one side. After several tries, Donald said, "I'll start the main motor and tow you to shore. Move farther around to the side of the boat so the motor prop doesn't hit you."

It seemed like forever before Don got the motor going and dragged me to shore. I was thoroughly soaked, from my shoes to the top of my head. Somewhere in the depths of Gilbert Lake, I had lost my cap. I was cold and getting colder. I knew I was a candidate for hypothermia. I took off my soaked winter jacket and tried to shake out some of the water. It didn't help. I put it back on. "We got to get you warmed up," Donald said, real concern in his voice.

My memory of what happened next is a blur. Donald helped me back into the boat and motored across the lake to where his truck and trailer were parked. He got me into the truck and cranked up the heater to the point that my soaked clothing began to steam.

"Are you ok?" he kept asking me as he drove back to my cabin.

"I'm all right," I said. Donald later told me he thought I might have a heart attack from the shock.

Later that afternoon, Donald stopped by my cabin to see if I was okay. I was quite comfortable, as I had started a fire in the wood stove, and it was toasty warm in the cabin. Dollar bills, credit cards, and assorted membership cards—the contents of my wallet—were laid out on the kitchen table, drying.

"I ruined an opening day," I said. "Really ruined it."

"Yup, you did. But what a story I have to tell," he said, smiling.

BOUNDARY WATERS NEAR-DISASTER

The Boundary Waters' remoteness is what makes it special. But the risks of being out on the water are compounded by the fact that help is far away. Steve and I had a close call on our annual fishing and camping trip in September 2002, when I was sixty-eight and Steve thirty-nine.

We woke the morning of September 3 to a stiff northwest breeze. We had driven up from Madison the previous day and spent the night at the Super 8 in Grand Marais. Now we drove to McFarland Lake, arriving about 8 a.m., and put in our canoe loaded with camping and fishing equipment. Our plan was to camp at Pine Lake, but first we had to paddle the length of McFarland. The wind was now up to forty miles per hour and kicking up good-sized waves. After a tough hour and a half of paddling, we reached the portage to Pine Lake, one of the largest lakes in the Boundary Waters, about seven and half miles long. On this day the Pine had waves with whitecaps. I suggested to Steve that we wait until the wind died down. Steve said, "No problem. We can make it."

We started paddling into the wind and waves. Water splashed over the front of the canoe. I began to wonder if I should have been a bit more forceful in my suggestion that we wait out the wind before trying to cross Pine Lake. Water was collecting in the bottom of the canoe. Luckily, we were paddling into the wind, and the canoe seemed to move through the waves with little wobble or wiggle. I made sure my life vest was properly fastened. I suggested Steve check his as well.

Once we were nearly across the lake, we could paddle fairly close to shore on the way to our campsite, now about a half mile or so ahead of us. The waves pounding the rocky shore made a roaring sound—so loud that any conversation between Steve in the back of the canoe and me in the front was nearly impossible. And then it happened: a huge wave splashed over the side of the canoe and tipped us over. I found myself in the chilly water of Pine Lake. I looked for Steve and saw he had been dumped out too. Thankfully, we were close enough to shore that we could stand on the bottom. The big problem was our gear: most of it was floating in the water around us. Steve yelled, "We have to keep the canoe from the crashing onto the rocks and wrecking!" We got ourselves and our canoe to shore and hauled our soggy selves out of the water.

We had made a bad mistake, attempting to paddle in rough water. Even worse, we hadn't put all of our gear in waterproof bags and containers, so many of our things were wet, including my journal and the Sigurd Olson book that I had planned to read when I wasn't fishing. Only our food and clothing were in waterproof containers. We managed to gather all of our gear as the waves pounded the rocks. Steve pulled the canoe far enough on shore so the waves couldn't crash it against the rocks. He tied the canoe rope to a tree. But there we were, a half mile from our camp, stranded on the rocks, with waves pounding a message of "stay off the lake."

We were wet clear through. Thankfully, the temperature was in the high sixties, so I wasn't worried about hypothermia as I sat on a rock bathed in sunshine. What should we do? We couldn't camp here on the rocky shore. Steve packed much of our equipment and supplies into a backpack and set off through the thick and hilly woods for our campsite, which we could see in the distance.

In an hour he was back, filling up his backpack again, and he suggested I fill mine and follow him along the rough trail he had made through the woods. The sound of the waves crashing on shore to our right made it too loud for us to talk, and we plodded on. In less than a half hour, we arrived at our campsite, a beautiful spot well above the lake's crashing waves.

"I think we'll be fine," Steve said. "We can set up camp and wait for the wind to die down. When it does, I'll walk back and fetch the canoe."

We laid our wet things out on rocks, set up our tent, and soon had coffee brewing. We changed into dry clothes and spent the rest of the afternoon watching the lake and listening to the waves make music with the rocks.

The following morning the wind had gone down. Steve walked back for the canoe, and soon I saw him paddling along on the lake's now glassy surface, smiling from ear to ear. The rest of the week was uneventful. We caught a few fish each day and had a great time exploring the nooks and crannies around the lake. And we had a super story to share with the folks back home.

~ FISH TALE ~

Unexpected Fishing Hazard

My brother Darrel tells a story that proves that not all the dangers associated with fishing have to do with boats, water, weather—or even fish.

Donald and I rode our bikes past Allan Davis's farm and to the end of his property, where we stashed them in an opening in the field hidden from the road by trees and brush. Then we walked across the fields down to the very beginnings of the Pine River, where often the river was underground. It was one of the first really nice warm days in late spring. As we walked through the marshland, the terrain became difficult to maneuver. Hummocks of dead grass rose nearly eighteen inches above the soil, and the spaces between were filled with water. Carefully we kept going farther and farther toward an open part of the creek. Then we saw a large pine snake (or fox snake) slithering off to the side. I hated them and immediately fell in behind Donald, trying to step on the same places he did. Then there were a couple more snakes—and then we suddenly realized we were in the middle of a snake convention! There were snakes everywhere, hundreds of snakes, and we were totally surrounded by them. A scene in the movie *Raiders of the Lost Ark* reminded me in later years what it was like. (I nearly left the movie theater.)

Getting to the open stream was not easy because of the rough terrain. Finally, we were at the creek. I was so scared I don't believe I ever dropped my fishing line in the water. Don attempted to fish, but he, too, was uncomfortable because everywhere we looked there were snakes. The most disconcerting thing was they just kept swimming down the stream right over his fishing line. He finally said, "Let's get out of here!" That was the best news of the day, since I wasn't about to leave by myself. Snakes slithered everywhere. At one point, Don grabbed a snake and threw it toward me. I couldn't believe that he wasn't scared. I was sure he did this because he knew I was so scared I could hardly move, and he made the point that in this situation, he was the boss! Years later he told me he was just as scared as I was. We were glad to return to our bikes and get home. We seldom talked about this experience because it seemed so far-fetched and we felt our friends would think we were lying.

There was a sequel to the story. The next day my ankles and feet began to itch and turn red with a rash. I was highly allergic to poison ivy and obviously had been walking through it while I was trying to avoid the snakes. For nearly two weeks I couldn't put my shoes on because of the oozing and scab stages of ivy poisoning.

—Darrel Apps

16

Piscatorial Retreat

For several years in the 1970s and 1980s, when I was teaching at the University of Wisconsin–Madison, I took a group of my graduate students on what I called a "Piscatorial Retreat." It was a fishing trip, but for the unknowing who didn't take time to look up the word, it sounded like some kind of exotic graduate student experience. My graduate students came from all parts of the United States and Canada. Each year, at least two or three of them had never fished before. Sleeping overnight in a tent was also new to most.

The retreat took place on the opening day of fishing season, usually the first Saturday in May. My favorite place for the retreat was the Peshtigo River in northern Marinette County. We tent camped at McClintock Park, which offered minimum facilities: campsites, an outhouse, and a place to build a campfire.

The Peshtigo River is known for trout, especially rainbow trout. The water was cold, usually in the low forty degrees. The best way to fish the river is to wear rubber waders that come up to your chest. This allows the fisherman to be in the river, or, as one of my students once said, "To be one with the river."

I remember one trip when we started driving to Marinette County early Friday morning. Our goal: to catch brookies, rainbows, or perhaps a brown trout. A late spring snow wasn't something we had bargained for, but the Wednesday before opening day, it had snowed two inches in the north. We arrived at our campsite by midafternoon and set up camp with the remnants of the recent snowstorm in full view. We pitched our tents and organized our camp stove, cooler, and cast-iron frying pan.

One of the fellows in our group had never trout fished or camped. I knew what he was thinking from the look on his face: "You gotta be crazy to camp in a snowbank just so you can open the trout season on the Peshtigo."

Saturday morning came at 4:45 for our group of Peshtigo anglers, with the temperature well below freezing. It took real fishing dedication to crawl out of warm sleeping bags in pursuit of the elusive trout. I quickly pulled on three pairs of socks, long underwear, two pairs of pants, two wool shirts, and my winter parka complete with fur-lined hood. I stretched my waders over clothing that seemed like what I would wear ice fishing. We had heard from locals that the ice in the river had been out for nearly a month, but I couldn't believe it standing in the frigid water. Even the nightcrawlers were cold. As soon as the hook hit the water, the worm quit wiggling, paralyzed.

As the sun slowly crept up over the pines lining the river's bank, I shifted my spinning rod from hand to hand, putting the other in my pocket to keep it warm. I wished I could put my feet into my pockets. After thirty minutes in the river, they felt like two clubs dangling at the ends of stiff sticks, which I knew must be my legs.

It was an hour before I had a bite. I knew it was an hour because as I got colder, I looked at my watch more often and the more slowly time seemed to pass. A tug on my line changed all of that—except the fish got off and I had nothing. A clean miss. I tossed the line back in the same place. Another tug, and this time the fish was on. My rod tip was bending toward the water. I worked to regain my balance before trying to net this fighter.

I wasn't cold anymore. The hooked trout raced back and forth in the water. My mind was with filled with thoughts like, "Is this one of those 18-inchers that I know lurks in this river?" Then I saw the fish. Nothing to brag about in terms of size, but it was a real challenge nonetheless. I tried netting it a couple of times and missed; then I succeeded. It was a 10-inch brook trout, and it had done what fifteen pounds of clothing hadn't been able to do. I was warm.

That evening after dinner, we built a campfire, and as we watched the yellow flames licking at the pine wood, we listened to the river. A waterfall a few hundred yards upstream pounded the rocks and sent threads of water high into the air.

As we sat watching and listening to the rushing water, we swapped stories of fishing in Canada and North Dakota, and I got to know my students in a way I never would have in the classroom or my university office. They got to know me and one another—and themselves—better as well.

Another year I convinced a colleague, Professor Pat Boyle, to accompany my graduate students and me on our fishing retreat. It had been a cold spring. We all had warm sleeping bags, so we slept comfortably enough. I woke up one night to discover the inside of the tent was frigid and the tent roof was sagging. My first thought was that I hadn't tightened the tent's guy ropes well enough, but I looked outside and saw it was snowing hard. The snow was causing the tent roof to sag.

By the next morning, it had snowed three inches. When we crawled out of our tents at sunrise, we were greeted with a return to winter and a challenging day for fishing the Peshtigo. I immediately started a campfire, and soon everyone was gathered around it, warming their hands, front sides, and backsides. We scraped snow from the picnic tables, and I prepared breakfast using my sputtering propane camp stove.

We had come to fish, and fish we would. Some fished from shore, and some pulled on waders and stepped into the frigid river water. I was one of the wader crowd, but none of us were especially comfortable on this opening day of the season. With the temperature below freezing, the eyelets on my fishing rod froze, and I continually had to break the ice from them so my fishing line would move through them. Fishing was slow. I caught one trout, which was about the average for the rest of the group.

Professor Boyle, who had never been camping or fished for trout before, spent the entire day sitting by the campfire and gathering wood for the fire. He later told me that fishing when it was that cold was the dumbest thing he had ever done.

On our way home, one of my graduate students said, "Thank you for this trip. There is reading a book, and there is listening to classroom lectures, but sitting around a campfire with the music of the river in the background is something I will never forget. It reminded me that I need to slow down and appreciate the little things. Like the sound of a river in the night. It underlined for me that there is more to learning than academics."

Lake Michigan Fish Tales

Larry Wellenstein, whom you met on page 116, grew up near Lake Michigan. Here he shares more recollections of fishing on a Great Lake, insights about invasive fish species—and a few more Uncle Jim stories.

We lived along the shore of Lake Michigan near Lake Church, Wisconsin. Growing up, I loved going down to the beach in the morning with the sound of the gulls on the glistening stillness of the water before the waves began their daily journey. Eventually, I would learn to fish this marvelous body of water, but my parents and I knew that it is not where you venture foolishly. It requires not just a general knowledge of fishing but a deep respect for the changeable conditions of Lake Michigan.

Also required are knowledge of weather conditions and a hefty investment in rugged gear. While some are happy to cast their lines from shore or from a breakwater, most dedicated game fishing is done trolling from a boat. If you happen to be lucky enough to own one, you need to be able to handle it in times that can change in twenty minutes from glass smooth to eight-foot waves. Fishing from your own boat, out on the open water, can be a challenge. Doing it on your own is not recommended unless you really know the lake, the weather, and the capability of your boat, and you make an honest estimation of your ability to handle the boat in ways that your life may depend on. It is vastly different from boating on any of the thousands of Wisconsin's inland lakes.

Lake Michigan Fish Tales

One morning in 1968, after returning from college, I got up early and took a cup of coffee down to the beach, eager to see what changes this powerful lake had carved since I last was home. The first thing that caught my eye on this morning was a new boat lift on our beach, which had me puzzled—until I recognized that same 16-foot aluminum fishing boat that I had so desperately struggled to keep from taking me with it over the Sheboygan Marsh dam several years before. Now I knew why there were two Penn Trolling Rigs in dad's garage. It seemed that Uncle Jim was joining the latest popular Wisconsin sport, salmon fishing on Lake Michigan.

This was a few years after the stocking of the lake with salmon to feed on the prolific alewife that had entered through the St. Lawrence Seaway. The salmon had begun to pay off big time. They thrived on the alewife, cutting down on the foul-smelling piles that littered the beaches while also providing a boost to tourism, as every port town advertised charter boats that brought in clients eager to pay for the chance of landing a 10-pound coho, 35-pound chinook, or even a trophy brown or lake trout. Lake trout fishing, both commercial and recreational, had been successful until the late 1940s, when the sea lamprey all but eliminated lake trout in the Great Lakes. With their demise the alewife proliferated, but with the planting of salmon, fishing on the Great Lakes improved. The presence of Jim's boat lift was a side effect of this, and I realized it was only a matter of time before I was convinced to take part.

I managed to hold off for that summer, always finding a ready excuse for the expected Sunday afternoon invite. But by the next year, my uncle had become known locally as a good salmon fisherman, along with another uncle from my mother's side. Both had been pictured on covers of the *Ozaukee Press* displaying fish the size of which hadn't been seen in decades. I thought that this summer might be my last chance to do any fishing for quite a while. With the political and social upheaval of the late 1960s, anyone my age would be hard pressed to make dependable plans.

So, I finally said yes. Things started going well at the beginning. There wasn't a cloud in the sky. The air was still and warm. It was past noon, with barely a ripple on the surface as far as you could see. Perhaps I was old enough to be allowed to judge when to talk and what to say. Maybe I'd be offered a beer or even two if we were out long and doing well enough. Perhaps we had both learned to soften a bit over the years. My uncle seemed impressed with my willingness to go with him and the way I helped prepare the boat and equipment for launch. I let him know that my dad had shown me pictures of some of his catch and how it spoke to his obvious mastery in transitioning to the big lake. I complimented him on his new motor of an appropriate size for the lake and asked all manner of questions regarding how he went about achieving his success finding where to fish and how deep in this 333-mile-long lake.

Inquiring about where to expect to catch fish, I was told about temperatures, depths, available food, oxygenation of the water, cover, and expectations for where to find the correct combination of those things for fish. I learned that each fish is different. If you want lake trout, you need fairly deep water (depending on the time of the year) because they like water as cold as forty degrees. Chinook prefer forty-five degrees. That's not to say you won't find them in warmer waters if they have a reason to be there (such as food or a spawning bed). Like coho, steelhead, and brownies, you might find chinook closer to shore in fifty- to fifty-five-degree water. Brown trout can even be caught casting from shore. In other words, it all depends on many variables that can be anticipated only with experience.

Jim showed me the Herter's fish finder he brought along to assist him in locating fish. He had always trusted Herter's as his source for all his fishing and hunting equipment. As I pushed us out from the dock, Jim got the oars in place and the motor primed. I jumped in with a smile and rowed us past the shallow sandbar so he could lower the motor. Once clear of the two large boulders that came up to within a few feet of the surface that year, I untangled the anchor lines, stored the oars, and we were off heading northeast, cruising at about eighteen knots. It was a beautiful day on the lake.

Twice, Jim slowed the boat to a stop and used the depth finder. The first time we were at forty feet, and few bait fish were visible with the finder. "When trolling you will have more success," Jim stated, "if you look for a significant presence of the fish the salmon feed on rather than the salmon themselves."

With his usual sarcastic sense of humor, he said that otherwise you'd be looking all afternoon until you found the fish you wanted to catch, and that fish would lead you to the area where they normally would go to feed. "Why not troll your lure along at the depth where the bait fish are? There's a better chance of finding them that way," said Jim. Our second stop was at seventy feet, with a large school of small fish at about twenty-five feet. Jim said this was it. I temporarily anchored so he could tilt the cruising motor up and put down his trusty 5-horsepower motor that we nearly lost to the Sheboygan River. It was a Johnson Seahorse and was perfectly suited for the steady, slow speed required when trolling. It was also handy to have along in case the main motor quit when we were miles out in the lake.

Jim then set up two rods for himself with a heavy weight intended to take the line down to just above the school, with his flasher spoon trailing six feet behind. He set up another for me in similar fashion, and we placed the three rods in holders that were adjusted to not interfere with each other. . . .

When you are sitting in the sun on a windless day in July and the still surface reflects the sun back at you, it can get quite uncomfortable in an open aluminum boat. Even when trolling, we weren't going fast enough to generate a cooling breeze. To make matters worse, Jim's cooler still held only one beer and one sandwich for each of us. This cooler is also where he put any fish we caught, and so after the first one hit the deck (his), we celebrated the occasion by drinking that cold beer and eating the sandwich. Too bad the boat wasn't big enough to accommodate two coolers. After another hour with no further action, we went in search of another school of small fish and found one or perhaps the same school about a half mile farther out. We repeated the procedure. Jim set up and quickly connected again, this time with a nice 8-pounder. Neither of his fish were fighters, and he was able to grab them by the gills and boat them by himself. Nice and easy. By the time we had been out about three hours, I was thinking we were about done for the day when my line suddenly screamed off the reel and I had the presence of mind to set the hook and slowly tighten the drag. "Got one!" I yelled. While my rod was up, it was bent toward the horizon. Suddenly, Jim's voice was breaking though to me. "Wait, don't let him out too far, you're going to lose him!" he said as he cut the motor and tipped it up. And then: "You're not doing it right. I'll get him in for you. Give me the pole!"

With that, Jim grabbed the pole out of my hands, and the fish, having been given a reprieve during this exchange, started circling back toward the boat. My uncle reeled as fast as he could but couldn't catch up to the fish. He yelled at me to get his rods reeled in as fast as I could, or the lines would be tangled. I quickly took the one to the side the fish was moving and reeled it in. Finally, the fish passed and the line tightened, again screaming. Jim was fighting the fish, trying to slow it down. I got to his rod on the other side of the boat and began reeling that one in. Jim again yelled to hurry it up as the fish was turning back toward us and he was rapidly trying to reel in the slack.

"Get that line in. He's heading for the boat!" Just as I had the rod in and stowed, Jim took my place at the back of the boat and the line screamed again, but this time not as fast. The fish was wearing down. I thought maybe I'd get my rod back but no, Jim said, "Get the net and be ready to use it." I stood back watching as the fish made another pass and came back again. This all occurred probably in less than ten minutes, though it seemed much longer. Finally, there was no slack time in the last approach, Jim had gained control, and the fish was beat. Alongside the boat, the fish tried to dive a couple times but didn't get far. Finally, the fish came to the surface, so tired it almost lay on its side. Jim stood back a little and kept the rod at about 45 degrees in case the fish made a break for it. "Okay," he said. "Bring him in. Slip the net under him from behind." He needn't have said that, but I guess that was just in keeping with the rest of his performance. I had to get on the other side of Jim to get in position. I slowly slid the net vertically into the water along the side of the boat, the back of the net above the tail. I asked Jim if he was ready and then tilted the net as I moved it forward and up, gathering this spirited beauty in. Ten pounds of unquestionable determination to live.

Jim held the coho up for me to admire as he said, "Look at this beauty you caught. That's just the right size to eat, too, nice for filleting. Good job. Now that you've got one, we can call it a day." We tidied up the boat and motored back to his lift. My parents came down to see our catch, and Jim pulled out the biggest one. 'This is the one that Larry caught. It put up one hell of a fight." I said nothing about this until later, when I explained to my parents why this would be the last time I'd go fishing with Uncle Jim. And it was.

—Larry Wellenstein

17

Grandkid Stories

There is no better way to learn about nature than to be immersed in it. And for four generations of my family, we have found fishing to be one of the best ways to get kids out in nature. My dad enjoyed taking his grandchildren fishing, teaching them in his no-nonsense way how to thread a worm on a hook, what to do when their bobber sank out of sight, and, perhaps most important, teaching them patience. For fishing creates opportunities to learn about more than fish and how to catch them.

Along with fish and their various characteristics, fishing introduces children to the many other creatures that are often present: frogs, turtles, snakes, waterbirds and songbirds, all variety of insects. They'll encounter larger animals, too, along with their tracks, scat, and other clues about their lives and habits. I have observed white-tailed deer coming to the water to drink and once watched a moose swimming in a Boundary Waters lake while Steve and I were fishing not far away. These opportunities to not just observe the natural world but to interact with it—carefully and respectfully—teach children to value and protect our resources for everyone to enjoy.

Sharing the fun of fishing with a child is easy to do, requiring just a few simple items and access to a fishing spot. My daughter, Sue, who raised two boys and is a former elementary school teacher, notes, "Expensive fishing equipment isn't necessary. All a kid needs are a fishing pole, some fishline, and a hook with a worm. And a bobber! One of the most fun things about fishing when you're a kid is watching the bobber." Sue suggests organizing a small tackle box for children with lures, a spare bobber, and extra hooks. She also points out that "it's always fun for kids to see a little container of fish worms in the fridge, next to the food"—the promise of fun fishing times to come.

Just as my dad enjoyed taking my kids fishing, I've spent many a summer afternoon fishing with my grandkids and great-grandkids. I've taught them some of the fundamentals, but more important, I've tried to share the other lessons fishing has to offer: resilience, self-reliance, curiosity, patience, decision-making skills—and the value of occasionally slowing down, leaving their cell phones turned off, and connecting to nature. Here are some of my grandchildren's fishing memories.

NICK APPS

Nick was twenty-three and a senior at Western Colorado University in Gunnison, Colorado, when he shared these memories of some of his early fishing escapades.

"When we were staying at a resort on Lake George, Grandpa and I went out on a little rowboat. I was probably five years old. We fished for maybe three hours and didn't catch anything. But just before we started back to the cottage, I caught a decent-sized smallmouth bass. We were using worms for bait, and I was using a really old spinning rod. Catching that big fish was just awesome. It fought really hard. It jumped out of the water! I was so happy to catch that fish.

Nick in 2011.

"Almost every night when we were at the cabin, I went fishing with my fishing rod and a box of worms. I caught mostly bluegills. In Colorado, where I grew up, I caught some huge rainbow trout—one time, a 25-incher. Once when I was fishing in the Boundary Waters, I caught a really big pike. It was super cool because a pike fights so hard.

"One of the important things I learned from fishing was the importance of patience—being willing to sit still and wait for something to happen. That's a good life lesson. I feel that a lot of people don't want to go fishing because they feel they don't have the time or patience for it. I think if these folks actually went fishing, they would change their perspective about it. When I go fishing today, I don't even care if I catch a fish. Walking toward the river when the sun is setting, looking at the cool surroundings when it is so peaceful, seeing a deer. It's all magical.

"Being directly involved with nature is good for your mental health. If you are on your phone all day, your brain is gonna change to mush and you are going to end up sad. For me, fishing is very therapeutic. I come back from fishing happy. It is so important to be outside as much as possible."

BEN HORMAN

Ben was twenty-six and working as a biomedical engineer for a firm in San Diego when he shared these fishing memories. (Once when my brother Donald told Ben the fish were biting, he turned and ran back to the car because he didn't want to be bitten by a fish.)

Ben in 2002.

"I remember our tackle boxes—my brother and I each had one. We each picked out our favorite things in the tackle box. Hooks, bobbers, lures. All the different colors, all the different shapes. Which kind of fish would be caught by which kind of lure. When we went to Lake George at Rhinelander, we always stopped at the farm to pick up our tackle boxes and fishing rods.

"One of my earliest memories of fishing is just before Josh and I went out in a boat on Lake George. I must have been in elementary school, and Josh and I were getting our tackle boxes ready on the dock. Grandpa had told us to be careful with the hooks on our fishing poles, so I was trying to grab my hook to secure it. Instead of catching it, the hook ended up sticking right in my thumb. I remember being a bit stunned but not feeling much pain. Since I didn't know what to do, I showed it to Grandpa, and he simply took it out and told me to 'be more careful.'

"For a couple of years at Lake George, we had a secluded cabin with our own pier. Near the pier was a little section of water covered with water lilies. You could cast almost anything there and hook a fish. That day we caught fish after fish after fish for an entire morning. They were tiny bluegills.

"Thinking about the main thing I learned from fishing, it is patience. The tendency is to cast the line over and over hoping that with each new cast, the lure will find a fish. Reel in the line, find a better spot. Now I realize the real purpose wasn't really to catch any fish, but to be in the out-of-doors. Fishing is a good way to connect to nature and to other people you are fishing with. Fishing a good way to connect across generations. You don't need a lot of physical skills, like you do for playing basketball, for example. Just watching the reflection of trees in water and seeing birds flying overhead helps me realize that I am a part of nature.

"Sometimes there is competition among anglers and deciding who is the better one because he or she caught the most fish or the biggest fish. But it really isn't about winning or losing, but about relationships with people and with nature.

"When you are out in nature, you are using all of your senses, smelling, hearing, touching, seeing, and sometimes even tasting. It is so much more than a virtual experience, which often includes only hearing and seeing. When I see a nature picture, I am reminded of the real nature that I experienced."

LIBBY APPS

Libby was eighteen and a student at Colorado Mountain College in Steamboat Springs when she shared these stories.

Libby in 2005.

"I was on vacation at Lake George near Rhinelander, on vacation with my family. I was probably six years old, and I was fishing with my brother, Nick. I hooked a big bullhead and pulled it out of the water. It was 10 or so inches long, pretty big for a little kid. I was happy because I caught a fish before my brother did. I picked it up and got stung by one its barbs located near its mouth. Surprised, I threw it at my brother. After the fish hit him, he—being older and bigger than me—threw me in the lake. I'm eighteen now, and I am still terrified of bullheads, because they sting and I don't want to get stung again.

"I love fishing. Fishing requires patience. Sitting on a pier, watching the sun set. It can take hours trying to catch a fish. I remembering sitting on a pier for two hours before I caught a fish. I remember the big island in Lake George, and what fun it was just to look at it. Sometimes loons were in the water, and I would watch them.

"Sometimes we need to say to kids, 'Put your phones down and go outside.' There is a great difference between that which is virtual, on a screen, and reality that you experience directly. That you see with your eyes. When you go outside, you smell many smells—after a rain, for example—that is the best smell ever. And the sounds, the call of a loon, water lapping on the beach—you just don't get that on your phone.

"What have I learned from fishing? I've learned the importance of patience. I've learned how to bait a hook and how to take a fish off the hook. I learned to be aware of my surroundings; if there are others around me, I don't want to accidently hook them. If there are ducks in the water, I must be careful with my casting so I don't hit them."

JOSH HORMAN

Josh was thirty and working as an attorney in Denver when he shared these fishing memories.

"In the summer of 2017, I'd just quit my job between college and law school. I went on a weeklong trip to the Boundary Waters with a couple of my buddies. Grandpa and I had gone to Dorn Hardware store, and he bought me a bunch of lures. We went to the west side of the Boundary Waters, right on the Canadian border. The first couple of days were quite miserable with rainy, cold weather. We were up there for five or six days, and we didn't catch anything. Two of the four of us caught one fish. Nobody caught two fish. The fish were not big enough to eat.

Josh in 2002.

"A couple weeks later, a college buddy of mine who had a boat invited me to fish with him on Mud Lake in Madison. My buddy showed me a picture of a massive muskie that he had recently caught. So, my buddy and I got into his boat, and soon we had a couple of lines in the water. We were out there no longer than twenty minutes and the fish starting biting. I caught a 24-inch northern. We had gone so many miles to the Boundary Waters, and here in the middle of Madison I catch this big northern, with the cars going by on the highway. When there was nobody around, we couldn't catch anything. When there were people all around, I caught this big fish.

"I remember as a little kid how difficult it was for me to just get a worm on the hook. I remember that Grandpa put the worms on our hooks, while showing us how to do it—hooking it in a couple places so it wouldn't fall off the hook. I remember fishing on a lake near Wautoma, catching bluegills. It was always exciting to see the bobbers go under, and my fishing pole bending."

CHRISTIAN APPS

Christian was twenty-five and working as a physical therapist in Colorado when he shared these stories.

"I have not been a great fan of fishing. The best story for me was in the Boundary Waters. As a kid it was more fun for me to cast than catch. It was fun to experience lake life in the Midwest. I live in Colorado with nature all around us, but the only water we have is the Colorado River. Very different from the lakes in Wisconsin. The Colorado River is very aggressive compared to flat-water lakes. You go to the Colorado River for adrenalin compared to

Christian in 2001.

going to a lake for serenity. . . . Here in the Midwest, I look at water to relax and be at peace. For me fishing is a way to pass the time. Fishing is a way to introduce people to nature and to the environment.

"Virtual study is one way of being introduced to nature, but there is nothing like the real thing where you can smell, feel, hear, see, and sometimes taste nature. When you are in nature, you are fully immersed. When you are fishing, you are acting in nature, which is really cool.

"Fishing helps kids learn to sit still and not be doing something all the time. Many kids are just waiting for the next thing to do. Fishing helps you clear your mind. Fishing helps kids learn what it means to be outside, for kids to create their own relationship with the outdoors."

~ FISH TALE ~

Never Too Young

When my great-grandson, Ty, was three years old, he had a fishing adventure that the family will never forget. His dad and mom, Shanna Bodilly and Pat Albersman, and his grandparents Dave and Deb Albersman were staying at a cottage on Minnesota's Lake Vermilion. They were planning to do some fishing, but unfortunately they had forgotten to bring along little Ty's fishing rod. What to do? Ty was set on fishing. Grandpa Dave had the answer. He found a small tree branch and tied on a four-foot length of string to which he had fastened a baited hook and a bobber. Ty could now fish off the pier with this homemade fishing pole.

Before his grandpa could say "you've got a bite," Ty's bobber disappeared and his makeshift pole began bending downward. Ty's dad, Pat, grabbed the string to help Ty pull in the fish, and soon they had it in the net. The fish was a 27-inch monster northern pike. Who says you've got to have a fancy fishing rod and an exotic lure to hook a big fish? Ty Albersman will show you how it's done.

Great-grandson Ty lands a big fish using a stick, a string, and a hook—and the assistance of his Grandpa Dave.
ALBERSMAN FAMILY PHOTO

Wisconsin Fish Festivals

Wisconsin loves its fish-related festivals, held throughout the year. Some are geared for competitive fishing, with anglers looking to break records for largest fish, most fish, and in the case of one festival (the Hancock Lions Club Fisheree), smallest fish. Others, particularly those held in summer, are celebrations of Wisconsin's fishing traditions and culture, offering entertainment, great food, and fun for all ages. Here is just a sampling of Wisconsin events that celebrate fish.

FISH DAYS, PORT WASHINGTON

Hundreds of people make an annual pilgrimage to Port Washington to honor fish. Twenty-five miles north of Milwaukee on the shores of Lake Michigan, Port Washington has hosted its fish festival since 1964.

Port Washington and other towns and cities bordering Lake Michigan once had a brisk commercial fishing business, but by the mid-1900s the industry had mostly died. In 1963, after a food poisoning scare caused many people to stop eating smoked fish, Port Washington's Smith Brothers commercial fishing enterprise organized a Smoked Fish Jamboree. There had been no cases of the smoked-fish botulism on the west shore of Lake Michigan, and Smith Brothers wanted to show that smoked fish were safe to eat. They invited food experts, politicians, and others to partake of smoked fish at their Port Washington restaurant.

Seeing the success of the event, community leaders decided to do something similar the following summer, and Fish Day was launched. The first Fish Day event included a parade, fishing derby, fireworks, entertainment, and many small food stands selling fish. Money earned at the event would go to charity. The festival was hugely successful and grew over time; once referred to as the "Largest One-Day Fish Fry in the World," it became a three-day event in 2023.[10]

MUSKY FEST, HAYWARD

Hayward, seventy miles southeast of Superior, is nestled in the heart of northern Wisconsin's vast constellation of lakes. It is home to the National Freshwater Fishing Hall of Fame—and its famous giant muskellunge, 145 feet long and four-and-a-half stories tall and made of fiberglass, concrete, and steel. Inside the fish is a Shrine to Anglers, which lists the world's freshwater fishing records.[11]

Hayward is also home to Musky Fest, a celebration of the musky (also spelled *muskie*) and of the North Woods' fishing history and culture. Held every year on the weekend following Father's Day, Musky Fest includes a fishing contest, live music and street dances, games, food and craft vendors, a parade, and the crowning of a Musky Festival Queen.[12]

WALLEYE WEEKEND, FOND DU LAC

Walleye Weekend began as a 1978 walleye tournament sponsored by Mercury Marine, a manufacturer of outboard motors based in Fond du Lac. The event evolved and expanded, and today more than fifty thousand people attend the free, family-friendly event held in Lakeside Park in June. Along with music, children's entertainment, a volleyball tournament, and the Walleye Run/Walk, the weekend features the Mercury National Walleye Tournament on Lake Winnebago.[13]

WISCONSIN CARP CHAMPIONSHIP AND TWO RIVERS CARP FEST

Launched in 2009, the Wisconsin Carp Championship is a sanctioned tournament that draws anglers from around the world to compete in Two Rivers on the first weekend in June. Held the same weekend, Carp Fest includes food, beverages, live music, and the carp tournament awards ceremony.[14]

KUSEL LAKE FISHEREE

The We Really Kare Fishing Club was established in Waushara County in 1983 to improve fish habitat in twelve Waushara County lakes. In early February, it sponsors a fisheree on Kusel Lake, five miles east of Wild Rose, with cash prizes for the largest fish caught.[15]

FUN ON THE FROZEN FLAMBEAU

Held each year in February, the Fun on the Frozen Flambeau ice fishing contest is held at Leonhard's Landing in Tony, Wisconsin, east of Ladysmith. The contest, organized by the Ladysmith Lions Club, includes raffles and more than twenty thousand dollars in prizes. Proceeds are used to improve recreational opportunities around the Dairyland Reservoir, an 1,870-acre lake in Rusk County.[16]

HANCOCK LIONS CLUB FISHEREE

The Hancock Lions Club knows that not everyone can catch a big fish. Some of us are destined for a fish on the other end of the scale—the smallest fish. This fisheree, held in January, offers cash prizes for both largest and smallest fish caught.

STURGEON SPECTACULAR, FOND DU LAC

Since 1991, Fond du Lac celebrates Wisconsin's oldest fish, the sturgeon, at its February Sturgeon Spectacular. The celebration takes place during the annual sturgeon spearing season on Lake Winnebago and includes activities on and off the ice: a parade, live music, ice carving and snow sculpting, curling and fat bike racing, and a sturgeon show-off station.[17]

Epilogue

I hope the stories gathered in this book have shown that along with the joy of being in a boat on a quiet lake, enjoying the outdoors, and anticipating the excitement of landing your first catch—maybe even a lunker—there is much more to fishing than catching fish. The more fish tales I collected from friends and family, the more convinced I became of the power of fishing to tie people together.

As we look to the future, it's clear that those who enjoy fishing will see dramatic shifts in how, when, and where we do it. For example, as climate change causes the waters of our lakes and rivers to warm, some fish that prefer cool water, such as walleyes, may disappear; those that thrive in warm waters, like black bass, may proliferate. Unless we all do more to fight climate change, the fishing we enjoy today may disappear entirely.

Fishing, both alone and with others, has been an important part of my life. From my very first fishing outing with my father, I have enjoyed catching fish, but perhaps more importantly I gained valuable insights about my relationship to nature. These lessons, often learned without realizing I was learning them, have been important to me throughout my life.

Jane Birr wrote this note after contributing one of her stories for this book: "I was thinking of asking all my family members and their kids to send me a fishing story that they remember and then I could compile them to share with our family. How fun would that be! Listening to you on PBS over the years has helped me appreciate the value of stories and how they connect us and keep us together."

FRIENDS OF SID BOYUM, COURTESY OF THE WISCONSIN HISTORICAL SOCIETY.
WHI IMAGE ID 123047

Acknowledgments

As with all of my books, many people helped me with this one. I always start with my wife, Ruth, who reads all of my work and finds errors that need correcting. A huge thank you to her for all of the time she has spent over many years helping me with my writing.

My twin brothers, Donald and Darrel, offered many stories of early days fishing with our father. My children, Susan, Steve, and Jeff, shared stories of fishing with me and with my dad, Herman, who loved fishing and showing kids how to do it.

Paul Bodilly, my son-in-law, provided stories and photos from his own fishing adventures and from some of his family members: his brothers John and Billy Bodilly, sister Jane Birr, brother-in-law Larry Wellenstein, and grandson Ty Albersman.

Thank you to my five grandchildren, Josh Horman, Ben Horman, Christian Apps, Nick Apps, and Libby Apps, for recalling their childhood fishing stories and sharing what fishing meant to them when they were growing up.

Bret Schultz, a longtime fly fisherman, shared some of his experiences fly fishing as well as an introduction to how to do it.

And finally, Kate Thompson with the Wisconsin Historical Society Press, my editor for many of my books, deserves a huge thank you.

FRIENDS OF SID BOYUM, COURTESY OF THE WISCONSIN HISTORICAL SOCIETY.
WHI IMAGE ID 123048

Source Notes

1. Information about fish species compiled with support from Wisconsin Department of Natural Resources, "Wisconsin's Fishes," dnr.wisconsin.gov/topic/Fishing/species.
2. Wisconsin Department of Natural Resources, "Smelt Runs on Lakes Michigan and Superior," dnr.wisconsin.gov/topic/Fishing/questions/smeltmichsup.html.
3. Bassmaster, "Bass Basics: Which Is Best, Live Bait or Lures," bassmaster.com.
4. Wisconsin Department of Natural Resources, "Winnebago System Sturgeon Fishing," dnr.wisconsin.gov/topic/Fishing/sturgeon.
5. Burnett County, Wisconsin, "State Record Sturgeon," burnettcowi.gov.
6. Fishing Booker, "How Weather Affects Fishing: All You Need to Know," fishingbooker.com/blog.
7. Travel Wisconsin, "A Brief History of the Wisconsin Fish Fry," www.travelwisconsin.com/article/restaurants/a-brief-history-of-the-wisconsin-fish-fry.
8. Mary Bergin, "The Story behind Wisconsin's Iconic Supper Clubs," www.travelwisconsin.com/article/supper-clubs/the-story-behind-wisconsins-iconic-supper-clubs.
9. Destination Door County, "The Tradition of the Fish Boil," www.doorcounty.com/newsletter/october-2016/our-door-county-the-tradition-of-the-fish-boil.
10. Doug Smith, "The Origins of Fish Day," www.geocities.ws/rooksmith/Fish_Day_Story.htm.
11. Marsha Weisiger, et al., "The Giant Muskie, National Freshwater Fishing Hall of Fame," Society of Architectural Historians, sah-archipedia.org/buildings/WI-01-SY1.
12. Musky Fest, muskyfest.com.
13. Fond du Lac Festivals, "Walleye Weekend 2024," walleyeweekend.com.
14. Manitowoc Area Convention & Visitors Bureau, "Two Rivers Carp Fest," manitowoc.info/event-details/two-rivers-carp-fest/2022-06-04.
15. "We Really Kare Fishing Club Fisheree Returns to Kusel Lake," *Waushara Argus*, January 4, 2024, www.wausharaargus.com/news-latest/we-really-kare-fishing-club-fisheree-returns-kusel-lake.

16. Rusk County Tourism, "Fun on the Frozen Flambeau," ruskcountywi.com/event/fun-on-the-frozen-flambeau/#.
17. Fond du Lac Festivals, "Sturgeon Spectacular & the Wisconsin State Snow Sculpting Championships," www.sturgeonspectacular.com.

Index

Please note that **bold** page numbers
in this index indicate illustrations.

Albersman, Dave, 152, **152**
Albersman, Deb, 152
Albersman, Pat, 152
Albersman, Ty, 152, **152**
Anderson farm, 30
Apps, Christian, **150,** 150–151
Apps, Darrel, **1,** 1–2, 14, 17–18, 25, **28,** 29, 31–32, 130–131
Apps, Donald, **1,** 1–2, 14–15, 25, **28,** 29, 31–32, 58, 87, **112,** 125–127
Apps, Harold, 15, 19
Apps, Herman, **v,** 1–2, 19–20, 25, 26–28, **28,** 31–32, **33,** 41, **47,** 58, 59–61, 62, 67–69, 85–86, **106,** 188
Apps, Jeff, 24, 39–43, **40,** 44–45, 46–49, **47,** 62, **157**
Apps, Libby, **147,** 147–148
Apps, Nick, 143–144, **144**
Apps, Steve, 34, 39–43, **40,** 44–45, 46–49, **47, 60,** 85–86, **157**
 Boundary Waters trips, 94–104, 127–129
Apps-Bodilly, Susan, 16, 39, 40–43, **42,** 44–45, 46–47, **60, 157**
Arnold (brother-in-law), 54–56
Austman, Helgi, 113–115

bait, 21, 72–79
bait and tackle shops, 73–74
baked fish recipe, 91
baked fish with bacon recipe, 91
bamboo *(Phyllostachus aurea),* 17–18

barometric pressure, 69
bass: largemouth and smallmouth, 4–5
bears, 98
beer-battered fried fish recipe, 92
Bergin, Mary, 89
Big Falls Flowage, 6
Big Green Lake, 12
Binkshank Lake, 95
Birr, Jane, 76–79, **79,** 110–111, 156
Bjoraker, Walt, 33–34
black crappies, 7
Black Lake, Michigan, 51
bluegills, 6–7, 48–49
boats
 author's aluminum boat, 32–33
 boat rental, 30, 32
 canoes, 33–35
 Grumman canoe, 34
 Johnson Seahorse, 139
 leaking boats, 31–32
 pontoon, 35
 and safety, 125–129
 Wenonah canoe, 35, **35**
Bodilly, John, 71
Bodilly, Paul, 71
Bodilly, Shanna, 152
Boundary Waters Canoe Area
 Wilderness (BWCAW), 94–104, 127–129, 144, 148
Boyle, Pat, 134–135
Boyum, Sid: illustrations, **5, 53, 64, 68, 75, 81, 121, 124, 158, 160**

163

brook trout, 11
brown trout, 10–11
bullheads, 6, 46–48, 147

campfires, 107–108
Canadian border and Boundary Waters, 94–104
cane poles, 17–18
Canoe Lake, 101
canoes, 33–35
  accidents, 128–129
carp, 155
casting, 122–123
casting rods, 18–20, 36
catfish, 5–6
catgut, 15
Chain O'Lake, 2, 13, 14, 41
Chapman, Lee, 113, 114–115
children
  grandkid stories, 142–151
  kids' first experiences, 39–45
chinook salmon, 12
Chippewa Flowage, 10
Christensen, Arnold, 25
Colorado River, 150–151
cooking fish, 88–93
  culinary traditions, 88–90
  recipes, 90–93
crankbait, 22
crappies, 7
Crystal Lake, 101

Dairyland Reservoir, 155
dangerous situations, 124–131
Davis, Allan, 130
Door County fish boil tradition, 89–90

earthworms, 21, 72
Ellison Bay, Wisconsin, 89
Embarass River, 50

fish
  nutritional value, 88
  species in Wisconsin, 4–12

fish boil tradition, 89–90
Fish Creek, Wisconsin, 89
Fish Day, Port Washington, 153–154
fish festivals, 153–155
fish fries, 88–89
fishing equipment, 17–20
  for ice fishing, 37–38
  for warm-weather fishing, 36–37
fishing rods, 18–20
fishing seasons, 52
  opening day stories, 52–58
fishing spots, 80–86
fishing terminology, 63–66
fishing weather, 67–70
Fish Pole Bamboo, 17–18
fly fishing, 74–75, 121–123
  fly rods, 19, 37
  fly-tying, 73–74, 122
Fond du Lac, Wisconsin
  Sturgeon Spectacular, 155
  Walleye Weekend, 154
Fox River, 50
Friday night fish fries, 88–89
fried fish, basic recipe, 90–91
friends, fishing with, 112–118
Fun on the Frozen Flambeau, 155

gaff hooks, 37
game wardens, 15
Garrison Dam reservoir, North Dakota, 115
Gast, Robert, 19–20
Gilbert Lake, 67–68, 118, 125–127
Gile Flowage, 7
Great Lakes. *See also* Lake Michigan; Lake Superior
  chinook salmon, 12, 137
  lake trout, 11–12, 137
  smelt, 8
  trout and salmon, 137
Great Lakes Salmon and Trout Stamp, 11
Green Bay, 7

Index

Hancock Lions Club Fisheree, 153, 155
Handrich's Hill, 70
hatcheries, 12, 50, 58
Hayward, Musky Fest, 154
Helen Lake, 116–118
Herter's fish finder, 138
High Lake, 10
Horman, Ben, **145**, 145–146
Horman, Josh, **9**, 148–150, **149**
Hotz, Dick, 17–18
Hotz's Hardware (Wild Rose), 17
Hudziak, Helen, 29
hypothermia, 126, 128

ice augers, 37
ice chisels, 37, 105
ice fishing, 25–29, **28**, 105–107
   campfires, 107–108
   equipment for, 37–38
   Jane Birr's story, 110–111
   river ice fishing, 108–109
   Round Lake, 59–61
   and sluggish fish, 70
ice strainers, 38

jig poles, 38, 60
John's Lake, 97–98
Johnsrud, Myron, 115–116
Jones, Milton, 69

Kolka, David, **28**, 29
Kolka, Frank, **28**
Kolka, Jim, 29
Kusel Lake Fisheree, 155

Lackelt, Henry, 13
Lake Butte des Mortes, 51
Lake Church, Wisconsin, 136
Lake George, 44, 82–83, 143, 145, 147
Lake Hilbert, 76, 110–111
Lake Michigan, 8, 11, 12
   Larry Wellenstein's stories, 136–141

Lake Poygan, 51
Lake Puckaway, 9
Lake Ripley, 4
Lake St. George, 113–115
Lake Superior, 8
lake trout, 11–12
Lake Winnebago, 8, 50–51
   Mercury National Walleye Tournament, 154
Lake Winneconne, 51
landing nets, 37
language of fishing, 63–66
largemouth bass, 4
leaders, 37
leeches, 72
Leonhard's Landing, 155
life vests, 126
Little Green Lake, 6
lures, artificial, 21–23, 24

"marl holes," 30–31, 85
McClintock Park, 132
McFarland Lake, 127
mealworms, 72
Menominee County, 115
mercury contamination, 88
Mercury National Walleye Tournament, 154
Minnesota, Boundary Waters. *See* Boundary Waters Canoe Area Wilderness (BWCAW)
minnows, 21, 72
Mississippi River, 6, 8
   ice fishing, 108–109
Mt. Morris Lake, 25–26, 27, 29, 53, 105, 107–108
Mud Lake, **9**, 149
Mushinski, Bobby, 69
muskellunge (muskie), 9–10
Musky Fest, Hayward, 154

National Freshwater Fishing Hall of Fame, 154

National Wilderness Preservation
    System, 94
Nelson, John, 29
Nelson, Ron, 29
nets, 8, 37, 141
nightcrawlers, 72, 74–76
northern pike, 8–9, 144
Norwegian Lake, 14–15, 30–31, 48,
    85–87
Nova Tackle shop, 73–74

Olson, Burton, 108–109
Olson, Sigurd, 128
opening day stories, 52–58
otters, 101
Outdoor Notebook (newspaper
    column), 3
Owl Lake, 96

patience, 3, 42–43, 144, 146, 148
perch, 7–8
Peshtigo River, 56–57, 84–85
    Piscatorial Retreat, 132–135
pickled fish recipe, 92–93, **93**
pike, 8–9, 144
Pike Lake, 98
Pine Lake, 101, 102, 127–128
Pine River, 69, 130
Piscatorial Retreat (University of
    Wisconsin), 132–135
polychlorinated biphenyls (PCBs), 88
pontoon boats, 35
Port Washington, Fish Day, 153–154
Prairie River, 11
pumpkinseeds, 7

quiet time when fishing, 2, 82, 112

rainbow trout, 11
recipes
    baked fish, 91
    baked fish with bacon, 91
    basic fried fish, 90–91
    beer-battered fried fish, 92

pickled fish, 92–93, **93**
reels, 37
Rhinelander, Wisconsin, 82–83
river ice fishing, 108–109
rods, 18–19, 122
    for fly fishing, 37, 122
    spinning rods, 19–20, 37
Roshara (farm), 54–55
Round Lake, 59–61
Rusk County, Wisconsin, 155

safety, 124–131
salmon
    chinook salmon, 12
    in Lake Michigan, 137
Schultz, Bret, 121–123
shanties, 26–28, 37, **38**
Sheboygan Marsh, 137
Sheboygan River, 120
Silver Lake, 7
sinkers, 38
sleigh coupe, 26–28, **28**
smallmouth bass, 4–5
smelt, 8
Smoked Fish Jamboree,
    Port Washington, 153
snakes, 130–131
snapping turtles, 97
spearfishing, 51
spinning rods, 19–20, 37
squirrel tails, 73
stamps, postage, 11
St. Mary's of Lake Church, 120
stocking of fish
    chinook salmon, 12, 137
    from hatcheries, 58
    lake trout, 12
    muskie, 9
    rainbow trout, 11
    walleye, 10
stormy conditions, 69–70
sturgeon, 50–51
Sturgeon Spectacular, Fond du Lac,
    155

Index

sunfish, 41
tackle/tackle boxes, 37, 145
therapy, fishing as, 144, 156
tip-ups, 38, 60–61, 106–107
Tony, Wisconsin, 155
trout
    brook trout, 11
    brown trout, 10–11
    lake trout, 11–12
    Peshtigo as trout river, 84–85
    rainbow trout, 11
trout fishing, 80–81
Tuscarora Lake, 96
Two Rivers Carp Fest, 155

University of Wisconsin–Madison, 33, 94, 115
    Piscatorial Retreat, 132–135

Viking Grill, Ellison Bay, 89
virtual experiences vs. outdoors experiences, 146, 148, 151

walleye, 10
Walleye Weekend, Fond du Lac, 154
water temperature, 138
Waushara County, 155
waxworms, 72
weather and fishing, 67–70
    stormy conditions, 69–70
    windy conditions, 67–68, 71
Wellenstein, Larry, 119–120, 136–141
We Really Kare Fishing Club, 155
West Holden Church Cemetery, 14
Wheaties fish story contest, 21–22
White, Grace, 116–118
White, Maury, 116–118
White Birch Resort, Manitoba, 113
White Gull Inn, Fish Creek, 89
White Mound Park Lake, 6
Wild Rose, Wisconsin, 17, 58
Wild Rose Fish Hatchery, 50
Willow Creek, 55
Wilson Lake, 19

windy conditions, 67–68, 71
Winnebago River system, 50
Winnipeg, Manitoba, 113
Wisconsin
    fish festivals, 153–155
    fish species in, 4–12
Wisconsin Carp Championship, 155
Wisconsin Department of Natural Resources, 4, 51, 52, 88, 125
Wisconsin River, 6
Wolf River and Rapids, 50, 115–116

Yellow Lake, 51
yellow perch, 7–8
Yellowstone Lake, 24

About the Author

Jerry Apps was born and raised on a central Wisconsin farm. He learned how to fish from his father at a young age. He is a former county extension agent and is professor emeritus with the College of Agriculture and Life Sciences at the University of Wisconsin–Madison. Jerry is the author of more than forty fiction, nonfiction, and children's books with topics ranging from barns, one-room schools, cranberries, cucumbers, cheese factories, and the humor of mid-America to farming with horses and the Civilian Conservation Corps. He and his wife, Ruth, have three children, seven grandchildren, and two great-grandchildren. They divide their time between their home in Madison and their farm, Roshara, in Waushara County.

PHOTO BY STEVE APPS